To Rod, my ever patient and supportive husband.

To my children who wondered why the heck I was always in my office on my computer but who love and support me anyway.

I'm back …

INTRODUCTION TO

PSYCHOLOGY AND CULTURE

WHY CULTURE MATTERS

First Edition

Mia Palmer
Mesa Community College

Bassim Hamadeh, CEO and Publisher
Kassie Graves, Director of Acquisitions and Sales
Jamie Giganti, Senior Managing Editor
Miguel Macias, Senior Graphic Designer
Bob Farrell, Acquisitions Editor
Gem Rabanera, Project Editor
Alisa Munoz, Licensing Coordinator
Abbey Hastings, Associate Production Editor

Cover image: Copyright © Depositphotos/yuliang11.
        Copyright © Depositphotos/ZouZou.
        Copyright © Depositphotos/Rawpixel.
        Copyright © 2016 iStockphoto LP/powerofforever.
        Copyright © 2012 iStockphoto LP/dyana_by.
        Copyright © 2016 iStockphoto LP/aluxum.
        Copyright © 2016 iStockphoto LP/filipefrazao.

Printed in the United States of America

ISBN: 978-1-5165-1553-0 (pbk) / 978-1-5165-1554-7 (br)

Table of Contents

PREFACE

The study of cultural and cross-cultural psychology plays a crucial role in understanding human behavior and in the search for a "Global Psychology." This relatively new field of study continues to grow. Myriad texts have tackled this topic, and research continues to be done to find worldwide similarities and differences in the human population. As an instructor of multi-cultural psychology, I have enjoyed exploring these texts and sharing information and research with my students.

I began to face some obstacles (as did some of my colleagues) in choosing a text that would work for my particular class however. As I am limited on time with the students in the classroom, and am teaching a 100-level course, I wanted to glean the elemental concepts but had trouble as each text has significant differences. I found that one text explains one principle well while another does a great job of highlighting a different concept. One or two texts go into detail to discuss research findings related to psychology and culture, and other texts may not mention these research results at all. Furthermore, the amount of reading and advanced material presented in some texts was overwhelming to some students who were new to the study of cultural psychology.

In order to make the course an *introduction* to psychology and culture, I found it necessary to use information from several different sources. One of the main complaints I hear from students is that some textbooks they purchase are left to collect dust as the instructor requires the text but does not implement it in the course. There have been many semesters that I required no textbook at all. This, however, is also less than ideal as there are students who like to read on their own. For this reason, I wanted to offer an affordable text that covers the basic concepts in psychology and culture that would actually be put to good use.

Every semester I have several international students who are still learning the language. I love my international students! What a GREAT opportunity to learn from them in a course such as this. Most of them are willing to share their personal perceptions on the phenomena in which we highlight. When the language in the text is more simplified and the concepts presented more clearly, the international students are able to learn more effectively.

One of the greatest challenges I faced while writing this text was the temptation to go to a deeper level with each concept. I find this subject fascinating and didn't want to cheat any of the students out of great information, but I feel confident that by keeping the concepts at an introductory level, many of the students, (whether English is their second language or they are enrolled in psychology and culture as a new student) will benefit from the style of this book.

A unique benefit of this text is that additional articles and documentaries that help clarify important concepts are added right along with the reading. The students may use their smart-devices to access the clips with the use of QR codes. In the digital version, which is also available for purchase, there are links available to access the videos and articles.

In this text, I have added material from those who have done extensive research and writing in the field of cultural psychology. I have included quotes, tables, and readings from those who have extensive knowledge in specific areas. For example, when we discuss culture and emotion, I present the research done by David Matsumoto and colleagues. When we discuss mate preferences and gender roles, I insert Hofstede's findings. Throughout the text, I have added readings of those from whom we can learn the best. I have also integrated the different styles of several authors; for example, Jeffrey Mio and colleagues wrote a text highlighting the personal experiences of those who live in different cultures and are adjusting to new ways of life. Shiraev and Levy have added vignettes (two or three that I have included in this text) to each chapter to highlight the principle being discussed.

I want to allow the students to use the knowledge they gain to their personal advantage. How can the things they learn be applied to their own lives? They should pause and ask themselves questions such as: "What does this mean to me?" I have included, in most chapters, an opportunity for the students to reflect on their own situations by asking specific questions related to the topic in the chapter. What are their thoughts and perceptions, and why are they similar or different from the perception of others?

I have no doubt that this text will at the very least, be a welcomed change for my own students who from my experience have appreciated the simplicity of the main principles in this course. They will not be overwhelmed by reading through large amounts of information or tricky vocabulary, which may have a place for the advanced student in this field but be challenging for students who are new to this field of study.

INTRODUCTION

The chapters in this book cover the basic concepts in psychology and culture. I understand that what the "basic" principles are in this field may differ depending on whom you ask. I analyzed six different texts over the last several years. While there were many differences, I focused on the similarities and concepts they shared.

I want to take an opportunity in this introduction to highlight the positive aspects of this text, its unique features, and why this style may be more beneficial for many students. They include:

- An INTRODUCTION of psychology and culture highlighting main concepts and research pertinent to this field;

- Compilation of the positive aspects of several different authors who specialize in certain areas of the field;

- More affordable text;

- Easier to understand explanations and vocabulary for ELL (English Language Learner) students and lower division college students;

- Embedded video clips/documentaries and articles available with QR codes for smart devices or direct links for the digital version of the text;

- "What does this mean to me?" sidebars where students can pause and relate learned information to their own lives to encourage personal awareness; and

- Personal experiences and vignettes to clarify and highlight concepts.

While they are not included at this point, there are a couple of areas that I feel are lacking in this area of psychology. They are the cultural aspects of death and grieving, digital technology and its impact on cultures, and marriage, love and relationships around the globe. I will analyze research done in these areas, and as I've done with the other chapters in this text, highlight the main research results and opinions of experts in those areas.

I look forward to the benefits of an introductory text in a subject that I love to study and that is interesting to so many others. I hope that my students will enjoy having a text to coincide with what I've been focusing on in the classroom. The greatest goal in the study of psychology and culture is to be aware of our own thoughts and behaviors while becoming more aware of the cultural worldviews of others. When we learn about other cultures and we take steps to improve interactions with those from around the world, we improve our own lives and the lives of others in our ever increasing global atmosphere.

Chapter 1

Why Does Culture Matter?

We are at almost every point of our day, immersed in cultural diversity; faces,
clothes, smells, attitude, traditions, behaviours, beliefs, rituals.

—Randa Abdel-Fattah

Figure 1.1

T he study of human thought and behavior has a very long history that can be traced
back to ancient Greece where philosophers such as Aristotle, Socrates, and Plato
began to enlighten minds and set the stage for western psychology and science.
It wasn't until the late 1800s that psychology emerged as a separate discipline. Wilhelm
Wundt, a German physiologist, physician, professor and philosopher, began to make the
connection between the biology of the brain and human thought and behavior. He realized
that certain aspects of human thoughts, emotions, and behaviors could actually be measured
and was inspired to open the first Psychology lab in Leipzig, Germany, in 1879. Opening

this lab was considered by many the beginning of modern psychology. It is for this reason that Wundt is credited as being the "Father of Psychology."

Great progress was made from the efforts of Wundt and his students in the newfound science of psychology. Students who worked under his supervision returned home to implement these new methods of research in their own countries. Insight was gained about the human mind, but only in certain parts of the world. Facts gathered about the nature of human thought and behavior were certainly not an accurate representation of the population around the globe. Therefore, numerous questions about human nature and the mind remained unanswered.

If human beings are all one people, belonging to one species, how can a discipline that thinks of itself as "the science of human behaviour" not be based on all human experience and knowledge?

—Berry

CULTURAL- AND CROSS-CULTURAL PSYCHOLOGY

Cross-Cultural Psychology began to find a way into mainstream psychology due to an increasing understanding that the thoughts, actions, and perspectives of an individual may vary greatly depending on the environment in which one is exposed. There was an abundance of information on individuals living in the Western part of the world (more specifically, college-aged students in America), but a much wider base of information was needed to truly understand ALL human experience. Cross-cultural psychology seeks to identify and comprehend both the similarities and differences of people's behaviors and experiences around the world. More importantly, this discipline offers the opportunity to connect with others through a deeper sense of appreciation and understanding. Cross-cultural psychology is the critical and comparative study of cultural effects on human psychology (Shiraev 2013). This comparative method includes participants from more than one cultural group which are compared for similarities and differences. How do people around the world differ in their emotions? Do we all feel the same? Do the same situations elicit the same emotions in another part of the world? These are just a few of many questions that can be answered by cross-cultural researchers. The final goal of cross-cultural psychology is to integrate what is universal and that which is culturally specific into a more broadly based universal psychology transferable to all cultures (Krum Krumov and Knud S. Larsen 2013).

How does cross-cultural psychology differ from **Cultural Psychology**? Cultural psychology attempts to find the links between a culture and the psychological aspects of individuals living within this culture (Shiraev 2013). Human behavior cannot be completely understood without researching the cultural context in which it occurs. For example, how do parenting styles, education, and religious ideologies in a particular culture affect personality traits and worldviews of the individual? Research findings on culture and its influence on an individual may or may not hold true to individuals in other cultures. Through both cultural and cross-cultural psychology, we can see similarities and differences with people and groups of people all over the world and consequently, gain a deeper insight into the human mind.

Culture has become an important aspect in our understanding of human behavior and has even become a selling point in our global world market. View the following bank advertisement. Why would this idea be appealing enough that some would choose to use this bank over another?

https://www.youtube.com/watch?v=WcEfzHB08QE

Krum Krumov and Knud S. Larsen in their book *Why Culture Matters* explain the goals of cross-cultural psychology and how our own *ethnocentric* views can play a role in our assessments of other cultures.

Reading 1.1

UNDERSTANDING CROSS-CULTURAL PSYCHOLOGY IN A CHANGING WORLD

Cross-cultural psychology has made scientific contributions in understanding human behavior as influenced by the cultural context. In cross-cultural psychology the variability but also the similarities of human behavior is of interest, as influenced by cultural factors, by common genetic inheritance, and by the similarity of human problems in the struggle for survival. Since cross-cultural psychology is a scientific enterprise we are interested in the systematic comparisons between populations under varying cultural situations in order to infer cause and affect relationships for important psychological dimensions. Underlying the interest in the variability in human cultural behavior is the finding that different cultural experiences with childrearing, cultural norms, and socio-economic institutions produce individuals that differ in predictable ways. In the final analysis cross-cultural psychology seeks to understand how culture affects the psychological life of individual human beings (Cole, 1996).

The above definition requires a more specific articulation of what constitutes culture as the term is used in many non-scientific ways. We can speak of people of high social economic standing as having "culture" which may simply mean they have the money to enjoy the good life and fine wine. Culture is also used to describe what is popular in society such as current fads in fashion or music. However, influential these ideas may be they are just a temporary phenomenon—here today but gone tomorrow.

Some researchers have used cross-national as synonymous for cross-cultural, however, cross-national studies can be carried out between culturally related groups like the Danes and the Dutch, and may tell us more about recent socio-economic changes and dynamics than lasting culture (Frijda & Jahoda, 1966). On the other hand, recent years have seen more studies on ethnic groups within nations. These groups seem justified for inclusion in cross-cultural studies as they often maintain particular cultural values over long time periods, and their adjustment to the dominant society is of obvious importance and utility.

Cross-cultural psychology is interested in inferring cause and effect relationships between cultural factors and subsequent behavior. Ultimately the objective is to develop a discipline where cultural variations are seen as antecedents to differences in human behavior by comparing cultural groups on salient psychological dimensions. In the process we become aware of what cultural experiences like language are salient and how these variables may be related to mental life and cognitive processes.

One important distinction is between the concepts of cultural and cross-cultural psychology (Berry, 2000; Poortinga, 1997). In cultural (indigenous) psychology an individual culture is studied at some depth in order to observe the relationship between cultural determinants and behavior. On the other hand, the cross-cultural (comparative) discipline seeks to study both the similarities and salient differences in psychological behavior and cognition between cultures. Research suggests that comparative differences occur because of socio-cultural factors, but also as noted from variability in ecological variables like climate, as well as biological factors. In both the cultural and cross-cultural domains we must remain conscious of the effects of rapid socio-economic and scientific change as cultural variables also respond to these forces.

THE MAJOR OBJECTIVES OF CROSS-CULTURAL PSYCHOLOGY

An important objective in the study of ethnic, cultural and national groups is to determine the validity of salient results and theories. To what extent are commonly accepted Western psychological theories actually *transferable* to other societies and cultures? Dawson (1971) suggested that the importance of cross-cultural research lies in the ability to evaluate the broader universal validity of psychological theories. More recently Segall, Dasen, Berry and Poortinga (1999) suggested that we should not consider any psychological principles as transferable in the absence of valid cross-cultural assessments.

Berry and Dasen (1974) outlined the major objectives for cross-cultural psychology. The first was called the "transport and test" goal where researchers ascertain whether established theories and research findings are valid in other cultural settings. The ultimate goal is to establish universal theories valid for all human beings. However, to reach such universal goals we have to start with what we know in our own culture and then test the validity of these research conclusions in the cross-cultural context. In that process it is also necessary to evaluate what is unique, and in particular the psychological variability and cultural specificity not apparent from our own cultural experience. If we cannot replicate common psychological research findings from our own society what are the reasons? For example, in human development adolescents typically go through a turbulent period known as "strum und drang." An important question could be posed whether adolescents in all societies go through a similar developmental process and whether there are unique cultural variations. The final goal of cross-cultural psychology is to integrate what is universal and that which is culturally specific into a more broadly based universal psychology transferable to all cultures. However, whether it is possible to develop universal laws of human behavior is a conclusion that not all investigators accept (Boesch, 1996).

THE ETHNOCENTRISM OF PSYCHOLOGY

Ethnocentrism is ubiquitous in the world. It affects preferential judgments of every kind including evaluations of religion, ideology, and culture. Children already at a very young age have preferences for their own cultural symbols, and view the world through the lenses of their internalized cultural values. Since ethnocentrism is at best a simplification it leads to many errors of judgment. Evaluating all important perspectives from that of one's own culture distorts the truth about other people, and does not take into account the full complexity of other cultures and societies. Unfortunately, ethnocentrism must necessarily also affect cross-cultural psychology. The very choice of what we study is based on the knowledge developed in our own culture, and most cross-cultural research choices seek to expand that knowledge into other groups and societies. Indigenous psychology would argue that topics not studied in the dominant Western based cross-cultural psychology are salient in other cultures. The psychological assessments we make are often based on concepts and instruments that have culturally specific meaning, and can only be translated at the risk of introducing concepts of little or no importance to other cultures. It requires careful translation as well as some evidence of cultural relevance before cross-cultural researchers can validly apply psychological assessments from one culture to another. Likewise the development of psychological theories in general is universally based on Western thought and data. Research based on Western theories applied in other cultures may contain ethnocentric bias and error.

However, these biases can be reduced by following careful procedures, and by inclusion of diverse cultures in the data base. Scientists are not immune from cultural bias and must be on alert for ethnocentric distortion in translation and conceptual development. Replication is needed to establish the validity of any psychological construct, and since times are changing psychological models must respond to these ubiquitous developments. Only over the long run through careful replication work can we be assured of a valid and reliable cross-cultural discipline. In recent decades some researchers have sought to develop a psychology from non-Western approaches. Although only modest research has been completed the development of indigenous psychological models may gather steam in the future (Sinha, 1997).

WORLDVIEW

How do we see the world? Our personal experiences have a large impact on how we view other groups and individuals across the globe. Physical environment, gender, social class, and sexual orientation are just a few of the factors that can play a role in our *worldview*.

A **worldview** is our philosophy on life or the way we perceive the world that affects the way we feel, think, behave, and how we interact with others. Part of understanding others from different cultures is pausing to make a personal assessment of our own worldview. We can ask ourselves questions such as "Why do I think and feel the way I do?" "How does my environment affect my decisions?" or "How has my family and everyday lifestyle influenced who I am?" This step to understanding ourselves and our position in the world will lend a hand in developing a more tolerant and understanding view of those around us, in the work place, while traveling, and more than likely, in our own neighborhood.

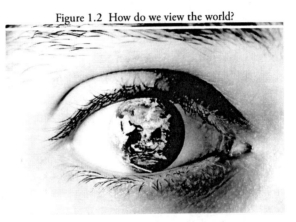

Figure 1.2 How do we view the world?

Copyright © Depositphotos/yekophotostudio.

IS OUR WORLD BECOMING SMALLER? THE PROS AND CONS OF GLOBALIZATION

Many of us have heard the saying "it's a small world." Why would people say this when obviously, it a very large place with millions of people spread to every corner? It may feel at times that the world is an overpowering and colossal structure where we may feel small and insignificant. Other times it may feel as if we are all living very close together in what seems like a small area. Finding connections between people can be exciting in an otherwise overwhelming population of individuals. There are conversations that may go something like this, "You're from Cameroon? Oh, my aunt lives there! Do you know her? Her name is …" There's a very small chance that a connection can be made, but on the rare occasion that it is, it seems to create a high level of elation and a more rapid and excited conversation to follow. It's something that we can share, discuss, and, as all humans want, feel validated and understood.

In recent years, the world has been made to feel even smaller with our ability to travel, use digital technology, and share lifestyle perspectives with many parts of the world. We are now able to view other parts of the world as if we are there; we have a window into the lives of others who used to be just in our imaginations. Now, we may have the *feeling* that we are more neighbors than strangers who are never seen. We have gained insight, and are continuing to do so, about all aspects of life around the world. We are becoming *globalized.* **Globalization** is the act of globalizing, which is extending to other parts of the world, by integrating and developing economies, philosophies, and lifestyles. This is yet another term that can be defined in many ways depending on what *type* of cultural aspects are merging. For the purpose of this introductory text, we will touch on the general aspects of globalization between cultures.

As is the case with every idea about human development, there are positive and negative outlooks on the idea of becoming a more globalized world. There are multiple perspectives of this "merging of cultures." What are some beneficial results of globalizing? The phrase "two heads are better than one" may come into play here. The sharing of ideas to improve our way of life seems like a terrific plan. More than likely, there will be an influx of knowledge along with tolerance and understanding about other viewpoints that cross many cultural boundaries. Furthermore, there can be great progress made economically as cultures come together to share resources, ideas, and global marketing.

WHAT DOES THIS MEAN TO ME?

In what way have you, your family, or your community been influenced by another culture? Perhaps there are things such as specific words, foods, clothing, or activities that were adopted from another culture that you were not previously aware of? If you or your family are from another culture, what activities or practices do you have that keep your culture alive? What are some ways that you may have influenced others around you?

••

Although there are positive results from globalization, there are concerns that cultures will lose what makes them distinct and unique. Traditional values may become less clear, and cultural practices may become lost in a sea of new information. Cultures may be influenced to change their ways of life when exposed to different lifestyles, gender roles, economics, religious practices, and even clothing. This is a real concern as cultures merge and create more universal ideas and practices. For this reason, some governments would prefer to limit the amount of exposure their citizens have with the outside world. The people of Hawaii have worried that their ways of life have been weakening due to an influx of several different cultures and eventually becoming a part of the United States. Many Hawaiian people have made it a priority to keep their culture alive through language, dance, and increased educa-

Figure 1.3 Where we are raised contributes to who we are and how we view the world.

Copyright © Depositphotos/rawpixel.

tion on the history and traditional practices of their indigenous ancestors.

CULTURE, NATIONALITY, ETHNICITY, AND RACE

Culture is a term that is used in many different ways in our written and verbal language. It also tends to be used interchangeably for other terms such as *race* and *nationality*. What makes the subject of culture even more complicated are the varied meanings each individual culture may assign to it! Most would agree that there is no "exact" definition of culture. Does culture mean art and food? Does it refer to ceremonial traditions or a group of people? A basic definition of culture is an information system with a set of behaviors, attitudes, and symbols that are unique to a large group and communicated from one generation to another. It allows for basic needs of survival, well-being, and the derivation of meaning from life. On the one hand, there are cultural norms that can be noticed *explicitly*, such as clothing or behavioral responses. On the other hand, there are characteristics of a culture that are *implicit* such as expectations for behavior, bargaining, or any unwritten norms in day-to-day behavior.

It is important to understand a few basic terms associated with cultural psychology. Words such as culture, race, ethnicity, and nationality (to name a few) can cause confusion. While there are some similarities, these specific terms vary in their meanings. Culture, as stated earlier, is a set of behaviors, attitudes, and symbols shared by a group of people and passed down from generation to generation. Let's explore a few more terms associated with the study of cultural psychology.

A **Nation** is defined as a group of people who share common geographical origin, history and language, and are unified as a political entity. It is an independent state that is recognized by other countries. (Shiraev 2013). When we see physical characteristics in an individual that differ from the local population, we may be tempted to ask, "What's your nationality?" If in America, the answer will often be, "I'm an American citizen just like you." This scenario can cause a person to feel like part of an "out-group" (a concept that will be discussed later) and separated from the "American" group because of a differing, outward appearance such as skin color or facial features. A student in the U.S. wrote about her experience:

> *I was born in America and have been a citizen here all my life. This doesn't change the fact that immediately when many people see me they stereotype me as a foreigner. I hate feeling like I am an outcast in my own home. If America is such a "melting pot" of cultures, why is it so hard to be accepted by the majority?*
>
> —Patrice, 20+-year-old Chinese American woman (Mio 2016)

Race is defined as genetically transmitted physical characteristics that a specific group of people share. The physical differences between groups of people have long been the cause of misunderstanding and hostility. Certain groups may share dark, straight hair while other groups have olive skin with dark eyes or lighter skin, hair, and eyes. It is these outward differences that can cause an individual to be immediately categorized and possibly treated in a particular manner. It's important to point out that while the majority of a certain race may share the same physical traits, there may be members of each so-called "race" that have physical traits more similar with someone outside of their group. For example, there may be a blonde-haired person who has frizzy hair, darker eyes, and more olive skin. There may be an African American who has smooth, long hair and light skin. Why are there what appear to be significant physical variations among humans? Experts have determined that in the early stages of human life, geographical location was the reason for these physical differences. Most people who live in a place with very little sun would tend to have lighter skin, hair, and eyes, for example. Conversely, those living in regions with a lot of sun may have developed darker skin to adjust to their environment. As time moved forward, race had become more of a social construct that was used to categorize people into certain groups. Many today still believe that these differences run much deeper biologically than they actually do.

Watch the following clip from "Race: The Power of an Illusion" that explains in more detail how race is a social construct and not based on biological differences.

https://www.youtube.com/watch?v=Y8MS6zubIaQ

http://www.youtube.com/watch?v=GyuKJAG11Cw

How has the idea or "illusion" of race contributed to misunderstanding and divisions among different groups of people around the world?

Culture versus ethnicity and race is explained in more detail by Krum Krumov and Knud S. Larsen. In addition, they explain how any group can have a "culture" depending on its history.

Reading 1.2

CULTURE VERSUS ETHNICITY AND RACE

Within a multicultural society like the United States the psychological variability between ethnic groups is perceived as caused by differences rooted in culture (Shiraev & Boyd, 2001). *Ethnicity* may refer to a common cultural heritage of immigrants even in the distant past and maintained by ethnic organizations in music and dance. Ethnic identity can also be found in recent immigrants who have maintained a cultural relationship. However, ethnic group membership should not be confused with national identity since there are several or many ethnic groups in most nations today. Furthermore, the borders of ethnic groups may overlap with several nations. It is also possible to have several national groups within an ethnic category creating complexities in the concept of national identity.

Ethnicity is defined as the possession of a common cultural heritage based on geographical origin, but also possessing similar language, religion and historical traditions. Ethnicity may for many people be another word for race. However, racial identification provides little useful information about the cultural context. The student of cross-cultural psychology needs to know what factors link ethnicity to psychological differences between people for example as observed in emotional display, cognition or motivation. Phinney (1996) suggested that for ethnic identity to have value specific links must be established between cultural norms and values and behavior. A related issue is the relative strength of ethnic identity. If the role of ethnicity is weak in the individual it is not likely to have much influence on behavior. In turn the strength of ethnic identity probably depends on the relative acceptance of the ethnic minority within the dominant society and the route of acculturation.

A nation, on the other hand, refers to people who not only share a common origin along with history and language, but are unified as a political state and recognized as such. That might seem too narrow a definition for some peoples like the Kurds that meet all the criteria of nationhood, for example, possess a relatively independent territory in the north of Iraq, but have members of the Kurdish nationality living also in both Iran and Turkey. Likewise the Palestinian people are by all rights an autonomous nation, and would have become a national state except by the imposed refugee status and occupation.

Countries have a culture based on their salient cultural history, their type of government, and economy. If the economic base does not meet minimal living requirements it produces a constant struggle for survival that influences the development of culture and the relative authoritarianism of governments. Increasingly because of globalization we observe the creation of cultural enclaves within sovereign countries. The Hispanic community in California, and the Vietnamese community in the U.S. created after the end of the war are but two examples from many that function within cultural enclaves.

Race is also considered an important social category for identity development although the physical characteristics thought by many people to be most important are of insignificant functional use in distinguishing between people on any meaningful psychological dimension. Rushton (1995) described race as based on a combination of heritable traits, but chiefly morphological characteristics that produce varying visual impressions. It is important to remember that in all races there are overlapping traits, for example, the red hair often associated with the Irish is also present in Afghanistan, and even some Africans have red hair. The different physical appearance of race has occurred because of regional isolation and the forces of evolution, and really has little functional value except for arbitrary evaluations and categories (Brace, 2005). *Race categorization* has created considerable conceptual confusion with some researchers proposing as many as 37 different races. Although most people recognize the physical characteristics of race these morphological traits are as noted of little importance in behavior.

The most important consideration with respect to race categorization is to remember there is always more within race category variability on any genetic based trait including blood groups (and also in other physiological indicators) than differences between groups. It has been argued that race is more of a social construct than one based on biology, and developed from the natural human need to organize and categorize the world (Hirschfield, 1996). Although there is little biological differentiation on the basis of genetic and other biological distinctions, race is a powerful social construct with many very real negative consequences from prejudice and discrimination (Smedley & Smedley, 2005). It is culture that determines attitudes toward racial categories and therefore the meaning of racial constructs.

ALL GROUPS WITH A SIGNIFICANT HISTORY HAVE CULTURE

All organizations with a history have cultural values. These values are often passed by the founder defining the normative context of behavior and ethics of the organization. Organizations take a variety of forms in modern society from political parties, to religious organizations or even gangs. All lasting groups have either explicit norms that govern behavior, or implicit rules that people conform to in order to stay a member.

The differences between males and females within societies are also reinforced by varying gender cultures. Gender roles generally define what society deems to be appropriate behavior. There are large differences in gender culture between fundamentalist societies and norms found in modern liberal countries. Gender roles are impacted by the history of the larger society, and what today is considered appropriate in one society (like nude bathing) may be the subject of severe sanction in another country. In some societies women have virtually no life outside the home, whereas in others particularly in the Scandinavian countries the genders are largely treated with equality both in the workplace and in society.

The term "popular culture" is also used frequently today to connote popular music and dominant fashions or other fads. Since these preferences exist within groups

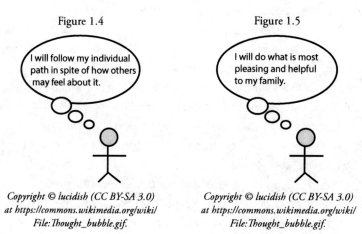

Figure 1.4

I will follow my individual path in spite of how others may feel about it.

Figure 1.5

I will do what is most pleasing and helpful to my family.

of people popular culture share some common features that have psychological consequences. For example, the psychedelic culture of the past produced musical preferences and in some case drug dependency and addiction. Keep in mind that part of any definition of culture is the persistence of behavior over time. Since musical preferences and popularity of expressions in fashion and arts often change with the passage of time the cultural influence is likely to be limited.

COLLECTIVISM VS. INDIVIDUALISM

One of the basic principles associated with cross-cultural psychology is the level to which a culture is *collectivistic* or *individualistic*. This is a very important concept because having knowledge of this basic idea can offer immediate insight into the actions of certain groups of people. Harry Triandis is the name most associated with the idea of collectivism and individualism. Triandis explains:

> Collectivism may be initially defined as a social pattern consisting of closely linked individuals who see themselves as part of one or more collectives (family, co-workers, tribe, nation); are primarily motivated by the norms of and duties imposed by those collectives; are willing to give priority to the goals of these collectives over their own personal goals; and emphasize their connectedness to members of these collectives. A preliminary definition of individualism is a social pattern that consists of loosely linked individuals who view themselves as independent of collectives; are primarily motivated by their own preferences, needs, rights, and the contracts they have established with others; give priority to their personal goals over the goals of others; emphasize rational analyses of the advantages and disadvantages to associating with others (Mio et al. 2016).

Our everyday thoughts and actions are influenced by a collectivistic or individualistic environment. The following are some statements that may be made by someone from each perspective.

Reading 1.3

Individualism—a social pattern in which individuals tend to be motivated by their own preferences, needs, and rights when they come into conflict with those of a group or collective in which the individual is a member.

Collectivism—a social pattern in which individuals tend to be motivated by the group's or collective's preferences, needs, and rights when they come into conflict with those of the individual.

As a way of measuring individualism and collectivism, Triandis asked people to rate the degree to which they agree with various statements that relate to the terms, such as the following:

a. One should live one's life independently of others.

b. It is important to me that I do my job better than others would do it.

c. My happiness depends very much on the happiness of those around me.

d. I would sacrifice an activity that I enjoy very much if my family did not approve of it.

If you agree with the first two statements, then you hold an individualistic perspective; if you agree with the second two statements, then you hold a collectivistic perspective.

A student discussed how her collectivistic upbringing can put a lot of pressure on her, but she did not feel that this pressure was burdensome:

My family breathes and lives on the words, "family always comes first—we must take care of each other." My parents have seen firsthand how the strength of a family can withstand any obstacle—these are not merely words of wisdom, it is a means of survival. To begin, my father immigrated from Mexico and my mother immigrated from El Salvador when they were both only eighteen years old. Even when she had nothing to her name and barely any food or clothes to wear, my mother would work days and nights only to be able to send money back to El Salvador for her mother and sisters. While her mother and sisters knew about how much she was struggling to make ends meet

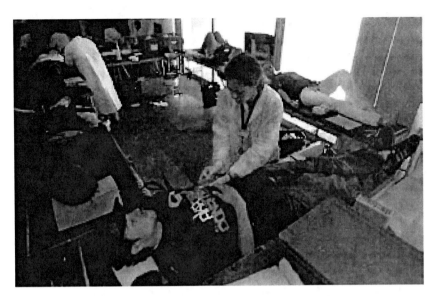

Collective behavior can help all. *Photograph by Tom Zasadzinski*

here in America, it was expected that my mother would send back almost 60% of her weekly checks back to El Salvador—because it was for the betterment of her family. With the money that she and her brothers were able to send back to El Salvador, her little sisters and mother were able to survive and were even able to send one of their sisters to school. Naturally, when I first heard this story as a little girl I asked her "why she would do so much for people that are so far away—and why couldn't they pay for their own things when you had to?" Her answer was simple and later I felt embarrassed for even questioning; she said calmly, "Because they are my family, and family always takes care of each other. And one day when you go to La Universidad we will all do the same for you. We will have to make sacrifices, but we will do it gladly so that you can make something of yourself; so that maybe one day you will be able to help us when we are old and tired." While this may sound like a lot of pressure to put on a little girl, it is not—simply because of the fact that these have been the same words that I have heard and lived by my entire life and I understand the role that I play for the betterment of my family; my parents have always led by example, and have done the same for us. My mother always says, "*En la union esta la esfuerza*," which translates to "in union there is strength."

—Jeannie, 20+-Year-Old Mexican/Salvadorian American Woman

Yet another student compared her collectivistic upbringing with some of her friends:

> Growing up in a Mexican and Sicilian home I was very much brought up in a collective society environment. Every action I made I thought about how will this affect my family. I still do as a grown woman. I used to get teased by my friends when I was younger endlessly for this. "Marissa, why do you let your family control your life?" my friend Rebecca would ask. I reply I didn't and thus an argument would ensue about how I was going to be a little girl my whole life. A lot of my friends who were mostly white didn't understand. Though, on the other side I didn't understand how they made decisions every day without thinking about their family first. If they wanted to do something they just did it. No questions asked, just freedom of their own choice.
>
> I was jealous at times but then I realized how close I was with my entire family including extended family and watched how my friends' families were not as close. They only had their immediate family unit. For the most part there was no value for their elders. They were put away in retirement homes while my grandmother lived with us. There was fighting over who would take care of their elderly; my family simply did it.... To me growing up in that collective unit was not suffocating but reassuring that I will always have people around me who love, respect and cherish who I am in this life and who I have yet to become.
>
> —Melissa, 20+-Year-Old Mexican/Sicilian American Woman

> Most people start by being collectivists, attached to their families. They become detached from them in different degrees and learn to be detached from collectives in different situations.
>
> —Harry Triandis, individualism-collectivism researcher

It's important to point out that no culture is ALL collectivistic or ALL individualistic but rather degrees of collectivism and individualism. Every culture has some degree of both. In the United States for example, we are considered an individualistic society along with several other industrialized nations, but due to the rising number of citizens from all over the world, it is not uncommon to see both lifestyles in practice. Religious ideologies, traditional family values, and location within a country may all have an influence on the degree of collectivism and individualism that a community or family may practice.

WHAT DO WE LEARN FROM CROSS-CULTURAL PSYCHOLOGY?

While studying psychology and culture, many students say that their eyes have been opened to their OWN thoughts and behaviors and how they have been shaped by their own cultural upbringing. One of the most important steps toward becoming more tolerant and under-standing of other cultural backgrounds is to first become aware of our own worldview and how our own culture impacts who we are. The following quote is one of my favorites with respect to seeing our world through new perspectives.

It's better to be a blind man who can see than a seeing man who is blind.

—Anonymous

We are learning from the day we are born about how we should behave, attitudes and feelings we should possess, and ways we should communicate with those in our immediate circles. We do this without even thinking about it because it's engrained in us—a part of our schema that formulates who we are as individuals. By studying human behavior around the world, we are better able to understand ourselves, the cultural worldviews of others, and improve our interpersonal relationships. We do this by developing our own culturally appro-priate attitudes and behaviors (Mio et. al. 2016). Our goal is to become multi-culturally competent. This added skill will benefit us wherever we are in the world.

Chapter 2

Cross-Cultural Research

Grieve not that men do not know you, grieve that you do not know men.
—Confucius (551–479 B.C.E.), Chinese Philosopher

Figure 2.1

Copyright © Depositphotos/Mazirama.

Obtaining data across the world to gain a deeper understanding of cultural psychology comes with some unique challenges. Just preparing to do a study can be overwhelming. One must research to do research! There are a multitude of scenarios to consider while planning to do scientific study abroad. The first issue that comes to mind for most of us is language. If participants speak a different language, one might ask, "So what's the big deal? Just have someone translate the information." That is more easily said than done! There may be words used in one language that simply cannot be translated without changing the meaning in a significant way. This situation can contribute to inaccurate data. In addition to the logistics involved with travel and lodging, other questions should be asked such as who are the research participants? Is it a random or representative sample? In what part of the country do the participants live? Are there strong gender roles? What is the local nonverbal communication style? Are the participants educated or illiterate? Will you need to use computers or any other types of electronics? Do you have the right equipment to gain access to the material you need? What type of government is found in the research area? The answers to all of these questions may have a sizeable impact on the research results.

CHALLENGES TO OBTAINING ACCURATE RESEARCH DATA

The following story from Shiraev and Levy's (2013) book *Cross-Cultural Psychology* is an example of one of the many hurdles that cross-cultural researchers may face when trying to collect accurate data from around the world.

Reading 2.1

Not long ago we were conducting a comparative Russian-American study on the perception of obedience. After we translated the survey questions from English to Russian, made a thousand copies of the questionnaire, and videotaped testing materials, we flew to Russia to gather our research data. We studied a wide variety of samples, from schoolchildren to construction workers, from engineers to psychology majors. There was only one problem. We needed to get access to Russian police officers but couldn't get permission from a county police chief. To our elation, however, after a few days of delays we finally were allowed to interview 100 police officers. We rushed to the police station, met with a local police chief, and handed him cash for "using" his officers as research subjects.

The procedure went well and when the last policeman had filled out the questionnaire, we went back to the chief's office to thank him for his assistance. "Oh, you are very welcome," he replied with a smile. "I really wanted to help you to get the best results. I told my lads"—he referred to the policemen—"to be serious and give you their best answers. I told them that it is a comparative study and that they should have

Eric B. Shiraev and David A. Levy, from "Methodology of Cross-Cultural Research," *Cross-Cultural Psychology: Critical Thinking and Contemporary Applications*, pp. 24–25. Copyright © 2013 by Taylor & Francis Group. Reprinted with permission.

given you the most decent answers."

We couldn't believe what he was saying to us! Did he really instruct his policemen to give us only "decent," that is, socially desirable answers? If that was the case, we could not have used the results of the study because all other U.S. and Russian subjects did not receive any instructions from their bosses about how to answer the questionnaire. And now, an officer tries to create a better image of Russian police officers and instructs his subordinates about how to answer questions!

This is perhaps one of the most common methodological problems of any comparative research: the subjects' attempts to present themselves as better than they usually are, assuming that their answers will be compared with their counterparts' surveys overseas. How could we have prevented such a situation? Perhaps we should have better hidden the fact that we were conducting a comparative research study. However, the next day one of our colleagues clarified the situation for us. He asked whether we knew why it took the police chief several days to give us the "green light" to conduct this research. When we said we didn't, he enlightened us. "The chief was making phone calls and gathering information about you and your research project. You did not have a chance to hide that this was a comparative study. Please don't blame yourself. That's the Russian environment: you have to second-guess and verify everything. The police chief did everything that he was supposed to do and any other cop in his place would have done the same. In a way, you had a representative sample."

As you can see, learning as much as you can about the country and specific culture where you plan to do research is imperative to the success of the study. Watch the following video to gain an appreciation for just how difficult it may be to obtain accurate information when researching in another culture.

http://www.youtube.com/watch?v=Oak03bdakOg

Figure 2.2 To gain the most accurate data in a research study, all factors influencing the results must be carefully analyzed for possible inconsistencies or biases.

Copyright © Depositphotos/a__n.

Because of the time and costs associated with cross-cultural research, it may be tempting to find a shortcut to reach conclusions. Research can be tedious and time consuming, but research done incorrectly the first time may have more negative consequences in the end. Because it can be difficult to obtain accurate research information, all research should be analyzed for any inconsistencies. One way to check for accuracy is to conduct a **Meta-Analysis.** This is done by combining the results from several independent studies, then comparing for disagreements in data, research biases, research methods used, and any other factors that contributed to the research conclusions. As critical thinkers, we should always question how research results were obtained and how they measure with other studies done previously.

THE "ETIC" AND "EMIC" OF RESEARCH

When researching human behavior between cultures, there are two main perspectives referred to as the *Etic* and *Emic* of research. Shiraev and Levy (2013) discuss this and other important principles in making cross-cultural comparisons.

Reading 2.2

COMPARING TWO PHENOMENA: SOME IMPORTANT PRINCIPLES

How similar are people in Tokyo and New York in terms of thoughts, emotions, and reasoning? Theoretically, there are two answers to this question, each one reflecting a distinct approach to cross-cultural psychology (Berry et al., 1992). Psychologists supporting the absolutist approach (often called the universalist approach) will argue that psychological phenomena are basically the same in all cultures: Honesty is honesty, sexual abuse is abuse, and depression is depression, no matter where, when, or how the researcher studies these and other psychological phenomena. Within this approach, there is a tendency to use the standards of one group as the norms for viewing other groups. From the absolutist perspective, psychological processes are expected to be consistent across different cultures. However, the occurrences of certain processes and behaviors may vary from culture to culture. A scientist, therefore, can study human activity from a position "outside," comparing different cultures and using similar criteria for such comparisons. Assessments of such characteristics are likely to be made using standard—for one country—psychological instruments and their translated versions. Evaluative comparisons can be frequently made from these assessments (Segall et al., 1999).

The second, the relativist approach, suggests that human behavior in its full complexity can be understood only within the context of the culture in which it occurs. Anthropologists were among the first to encourage psychologists not to use moral standards of one culture to judge others (Benedict, 1934). Therefore, the scientist should study an individual's psychology from within his culture. Since there are no context-free psychological processes or behaviors, valid comparisons cannot be made among cultures. In other words, from the relativist view practically any cross-cultural comparison is biased.

Quite often in cross-cultural literature, the reader will find the expressions "etic" and "emic." The term etic refers to the absolutist position, whereas emic stands for the relativist approach. As expected, it is difficult to find a psychologist who is a die-hard absolutist or relativist. Most cross-cultural psychologists today accept a view that combines these two approaches. Some phenomena in psychology are universal for all social groups, both large and small, including cultures and subcultures. However, there are psychological phenomena that are unique for only particular social and cultural conditions. Therefore, psychological comparative measures should be developed in culturally meaningful terms, and comparisons and interpretations of findings have to be made cautiously. This approach does not separate the etic and emic concepts. Instead, it somewhat interconnects them. One of the tasks of cross-cultural psychology then is to determine the balance between both universal and culturally specific characteristics of human behavior, emotion, motivation, and thought.

Even though the absolutist and relativist approaches seem to be dissimilar, they both make sense. Take, for example, the relativist standpoint on phenomenon such as greeting procedures. For anyone examining human communication across countries, it will soon become obvious that the rules of contact are quite different. In some cultures, such as the United States and Canada, a handshake is appropriate for both men and women. In Slavic countries, most women do not normally shake hands when they meet another person. In Northern Europe, men rarely kiss each other when they meet, whereas in the Middle East this type of greeting is appropriate. Direct eye contact is considered appropriate in many countries, with the exception of some East Asian cultures, where people, in most cases, greet each other with a bow, without eye contact. Even the distance of conversation varies substantially across countries and regions. Therefore, it is very difficult to study greeting styles in different cultures because in these cases, according to a U.S. expression, we would be comparing "apples to oranges."

The absolutist (universalist) approach is defendable too. Imagine yourself for a minute as a professional psychologist who studies physical and sexual abuse against women in a particular country. By studying cases, and conducting individual interviews, you uncover evidence that women in this country are abused to a significantly greater extent than U.S. women are. Some critics, that is, supporters of the relativist view, might suggest that your data are invalid because "American" views on abuse cannot be applied to other national samples. You, however, could argue that there is no such thing as "cultural" justification for abuse, as there should not be a "cultural" justification for violence and murder.

QUALITATIVE AND QUANTITATIVE RESEARCH

Research in cultural and multi-cultural psychology is typically divided into two main categories: quantitative and qualitative. Anytime something is measured, like distance, weight,

Figure 2.3 Human activities may be researched through measures of central tendency.

Figure 2.4 Research can use subjective methods such as observing others in a natural setting.

temperature, speed, etc., it involves quantity. As surprising as it may seem, these measurements can be used for human activities as well. It may prove to be a little more challenging when attempting to measure human thoughts or emotions because these things may be difficult to quantify. Still, there is a place for quantitative methodology when studying Psychology.

Choosing the correct measurement scale is crucial to the success of any psychological study (Shiraev 2013). **Quantitative methodology** includes **measures of central tendency**. There are three measures of central tendency: the *mode, median,* and *mean.* All of these methods are used in finding where score distributions are located. The measure of central tendency that is used the most often in cross-cultural research is the **mean**, which tells the researcher the mathematical central point of a distribution of scores; the most frequently occurring score in the data is the **mode**; and in simple terms, the **median** is the data that is at the 50th percentile. For example, if you want to find the socioeconomic status of the population in a country, you will have to find a point on the country's income distribution scale that indicates a 50 percent level. (Shiraev and Levy 2013).

Qualitative research is a more subjective approach to studying other cultures. These underlying, unspoken rules of behavior in a culture that can't be measured through quantitative means may be studied in a natural setting through qualitative research. The relationship between quantitative and qualitative methods in cross-cultural research is further explained by Krumov and Larsen (2013) in their book *Why Culture Matters*.

Reading 2.3

Qualitative research is dominant in cross-cultural anthropology. Social scientists trained in this tradition often have contempt for the research of quantitative psychologists feeling that they distort social reality and glimpse only small portions of relevant information in a culture. The attempt to build psychology up as a quantitative science probably derived from the widespread disbelief and reaction to speculative psychological analysis found in psychoanalysis and other subjective approaches. Behaviorism that followed, however, seemed unsatisfactory because it did not explain much of what went on subjectively, and largely established relationships between stimuli and responses. In reaction to these concerns subjective methods came into play in cultural psychology. *Qualitative methods are employed more in studies of singular cultures whereas quantitative methods are used more in the comparative approaches of cross-cultural psychology.* However, even in comparative approaches culturally specific qualities are not easily understood by using quantitative methods. It seems desirable to use both approaches to gradually understand that which is similar between cultures, and also that which is specific to each society.

Qualitative research emphasizes that cultural reality is socially constructed and to understand that reality requires a relationship between researcher and the culture studied (Denzin & Lincoln, 2000). Specifically the relationship in question is often between the researcher and trusted informants that are conversant with cultural values and normative behavior. From the qualitative perspective the research objective is to gradually build a complete holistic picture of the culture that provides the foundation for psychological regularities (Hwang, 2012). This objective requires that research is more broadly conducted in the natural environment, and cannot consist of paper and pencil instruments.

Qualitative methods in psychology include unstructured interviews where the researcher seeks to understand some general aspect of culture by starting conversations on topics of interest allowing the informant to respond in an open fashion and without structured constraints. Observations in the natural setting is an alternative approach that allows the coding of the observed behavior related to specific events like marriage ceremonies or the birth of a child. However, it should be stressed that spontaneous observation is of little utility. Although observation from a qualitative perspective occurs in the natural environment, the behavior of interest should focus on identifiable behaviors that can be measured at least by frequency of occurrence in order to evaluate its significance and salience. Observation requires a great deal of patience as it follows no specific time rule, and requires a willingness by the culturally identified individuals to tolerate being watched. However, the technique is most effective when the researcher becomes a participant observer, and gets included in the society observed. Interviews can also be recorded and subsequently coded for frequency of responses. When the culture has written traditions it is also possible to evaluate texts. The insight that the researcher possesses about the culture is of great importance in qualitative research, and if not present creates obvious validity problems. Theory development using qualitative research is an inductive process where the researcher gradually builds abstractions based on multiple sources (Charmaz, 1995; Silverman, 1993).

Content analysis is another qualitative approach. Typically the investigator gathers relevant documents and summarizes the manifest and latent content of the writing. A variety of written or performed material can prove useful including taped conversations, media programs, newspaper articles and books. The initial task of the researcher after studying the material is to establish coding categories. For example, if hostility is of interest the researcher may establish what words are associated with the concept and then count the frequency in a given communication. Next the investigator tries to interpret what the frequencies mean in the cultural context. The presence or the frequency of reference to the issue can provide important information about a cultural context that later can be investigated by means of hypothesis testing studies. However, there are situations when for legal or moral reasons subjects do not want to provide written material in which case the interview may be a more useful methodological strategy (Shiraev & Sobel, 2006).

From the perspective of qualitative research quantitative results are often seen as distortions of the underlying reality. However, there is no reason why both approaches cannot be employed as they are not antagonistic, but rather complementary. Qualitative research can be used in the initial exploratory stages to obtain familiarity with the context or explore for key determinants. Quantitative methods can build on this initial conceptual development and be used for comparative studies. The argument by qualitative researchers is that the complexity of cultural behavior can never be fully understood using quantitative means, but rather by first understanding the important contextual variables. In qualitative research the scientist seeks to understand the values of a culture not from a priori conceptions as seen from the outside, but in the terms of the conceptions existing in the culture. An obvious danger of quantitative research is that the constructs examined are developed from the framework of the culture of the researcher. The very objects of study and methods used in such comparative approaches can create bias in the data and interpretations.

The differences between qualitative and quantitative approaches are related to the historical divisions between emic and etic conceptions of research. From the emic approach research should only be conducted within a culture and researchers examine one culture at a time. The structural relationships discovered in the process and any criteria used to evaluate findings are developed from these internal characteristics. On the other hand, the etic approach seeks to understand cultural behavior from outside the cultural system studied and engages in comparative studies. In etic research the methodological structure employed is developed by the researcher, and evaluative criteria are based on the assumption of the universality of psychological phenomenon (Berry, 1969).

In practice both methods are employed in cross-cultural psychology. Segall, Dasen, Berry and Poortinga (1999) suggested that researchers start with an "imposed etic" by applying constructs developed outside the culture. As knowledge develops from the culturally comparative studies the researcher becomes more sensitive to the similarities with other cultures and also the culturally specific ones. Eventually, researchers may discover that the traits examined have universal features, and that other aspects are culture specific (Berry, 1969).

During this writer's work with the Aborigines in Australia a combination of these methods were used to understand fringe dwellers behavior, attitudes of whites toward Aborigines, discrimination, and alcohol related behaviors (Larsen, 1977, 1978a, 1978b, 1981). These studies were based first on subjective qualitative approaches, and then followed by more quantitative analysis. For example, to understand the domain of whites' attitudes toward aborigines the researcher first informally engaged patrons in conversation about Aborigines in a variety of natural settings like hotels and bars to collect statements that could represent the attitude universe. These were then edited and subsequently used in unidimensional scaling approaches.

BIAS, EQUIVALENCE, AND ETHNOCENTRISM IN RESEARCH

Let's assume that all of the conditions for a cultural study were perfect; all of the data was collected, and every activity involved with the research went exactly as planned. This is I'm sure, a wonderful feeling for any researcher trying to obtain valued information. Yet there still lies another hurdle at this point with any study. Who reads the data and how it is analyzed and recorded is a crucial step in completing a study in cross-cultural research and can greatly affect the conclusions made. There may be biases (or a state of nonequivalence) (Matsumoto and Juang 2013) involved on the part of the researchers when collecting and analyzing the research data.

Ethnocentrism can alter our views and assessments when studying another culture. When the observer's OWN ethnic, national, or cultural viewpoint supports his or her judgement about OTHER ethnic, national, or cultural groups' behaviors (Shiraev 2013), this is considered an *ethnocentric* viewpoint. For example, when sharing a meal with an Ethiopian family, I was surprised that we ate the entire meal with our right hands (use of the left hand is considered unsanitary and offensive in their culture). This way of eating at first, seemed unnatural and wrong. Is eating with your hands wrong? My immediate viewpoint that we shouldn't use our hands is an example of ethnocentrism. I was judging their idea of how one should consume a meal by what was natural and comfortable in my own culture.

Look at the following cartoon. This is a great example of two opposing perspectives. Each person feels just as strongly about her point of view. Who's right and who's wrong?

https://thesocietypages.org/socimages/files/2008/12/1.png

Krumov et al. (2013) discuss equivalence and bias in research studies in the following paragraphs.

Reading 2.4

CULTURAL BIAS AND CRITERION OF EQUIVALENCE

The most significant issue in cross-cultural research is the *equivalence* of comparative research concepts and methodology. Are the concepts employed in comparative research and the research methodology used equivalent in each culture? If the conceptual foundation and research methods are not similar it is not possible to draw comparative conclusions. The lack of equivalence will inevitably produce bias in the results and interpretations. Therefore a significant precursor to valid methodology is creating studies that meet the test of equivalence.

THE ISSUE OF LANGUAGE EQUIVALENCE

By its very nature cross-cultural research is often conducted with respondents who speak different languages. The first issue in comparative research therefore is to evaluate the equivalence of translations of the original research protocol. Whether the researcher employs surveys, attitude scales or interview protocols, linguistic equivalence is the first and most important condition of valid research. The development of research instruments should initially utilize multi-lingual participants (Van de Vijver & Hambleton, 1996). However, what happens in reality most frequently is that the research protocol is developed in the investigators culture and then translated into the language of those cultural groups selected for comparison. The first step in creating linguistic equivalence is to ask a committee of bilingual experts to collectively evaluate the research instrument. They will be asked to indicate their opinions as to whether the individual items or statements belong to the research domain selected. The experts will be asked to look for items that do not validly reflect cultural experience and whether a participating cultural group has a unique language context that affects the item responses. Language constructs that are culturally specific, and for which there is no equivalence in other cultures, would introduce bias. The committee of bilingual experts works toward a consensus about the appropriateness of the language used in the research protocol.

The second method used since the 1970s is called back translation (Brislin, 1970, 1993). The researchers have the research document translated into the other languages of interest, after which independent participants translate it back into the original language. If the retranslation is semantically equivalent to the original language protocol the researcher can have confidence in language equivalence. In other words a satisfactory criterion is met when the independent back translation produces more or less the original language used. The back translation procedure requires the participation of experts that are fluent in the languages employed. If the original form is found not to be translatable, the researcher must return to the drawing boards and use a different alternative language in the protocol. Since many participants in cross-cultural research are bilingual and often use English as a second language, researchers have to be cognizant of the possibility that responses are influenced by the participant's stereotypes of the culture of the particular language (Bond, 1983).

PSYCHOMETRIC EQUIVALENCE

The research instruments must also be developed in a manner that ensures measurement equivalence. A fundamental issue in evaluating *psychometric equivalence* is the degree to which the instruments used in the cultures participating in the research measure the same construct. If equivalence is attained the researcher should expect the same or similar order of preferences as measured by the use of response categories and the same order of item difficulty. Further, a criterion of equivalence is met when similar correlation patterns between items occur in comparisons between cultures. However, even where we have followed a valid translation procedure there is no way of knowing a priori if the language chosen in the research protocol has the same meaning in different societies (Poortinga, 1989). If the protocol means different things it is not possible to make valid comparisons.

Underlying all measurement concerns are the concepts of reliability and validity. Reliability is assessed by several methods, but refers essentially to whether the instrument elicits consistent responses internally or over time. Internal reliability is determined by intercorrelations that measure the degree to which items belong together. Significant intercorrelations are expected where measures have structural equivalence. Validity, on the other hand, asks the question of whether the research instrument measures what it purports to measure.

An important consideration is equivalence in the theoretical framework used or in the constructs being employed in the study. Comparability is impossible when the theoretical framework is not the same in comparison studies for example when the constructs measured mean different things depending on interpretation. Typically respondents in Western Europe or North America are guided by rationality in responding to psychological assessments. Responses of Western participants are mainly influenced by an educational system that reinforces rationality and rewards logical thinking. Other cultures may reward intuitive thinking processes and that difference makes comparisons of cultures difficult. Different thinking processes between cultures may result in measuring an aspect of the culture that confounds the variable of interest and makes analysis guarded.

Van de Vijver and Leung (1997a, b) suggested several types of linguistic equivalence. One approach asks whether the instrument measures the same underlying construct in the cultures examined. For example is the concept of intelligence the same in the comparative cultures, or does it depend on cultural uniqueness factors not measured? However, as noted above, a test of structural equivalence is found if the pattern of intercorrelations is the same or similar across cultures.

The underlying response structure in comparative studies can also be examined by means of factor analysis. A factor analysis with varimax rotation will allow the researcher to determine the level of factorial agreement. Factor analysis group survey items together based on item intercorrelations, and the factors are thought to represent different independent concepts. If the same group of items emerge in different cultural samples that is taken as evidence of structural similarity or structural equivalence. The similarity of the factor loadings is accepted as evidence of psychometric equivalence. Statistical techniques to further assist in evaluating psychometric equivalence include regression analysis that reports the amount of variance contributed by each variable to the construct. In the analysis of variance procedure it is also possible to examine for interaction between items and cultural effects, and where none are present that result is evidence of equivalence.

SELECTING EQUIVALENT SAMPLES IN CROSS-CULTURAL PSYCHOLOGY

The selection of comparative and representative samples is difficult in cross-cultural research because of the complexity of the variables studied and for the practical reasons that random samples are less accessible. Literacy rates and educational levels vary between societies and that heterogeneity may become a confounding factor in the response patterns of the participants. Further, the influence from travel and contacts that are by-products of a globalized world make it nearly impossible to obtain pure culturally influenced responses in today's world.

For practical reasons culture refers in many cross-cultural studies to the country of origin of the respondents. In effect cross-national studies often replace cross-cultural research. This imprecise definition defeats equivalence since as we noted in chapter 1 different ethnic groups and cultures can co-exist within a nation. In any event in cross-national studies care should be taken not to assume national homogeneity as even countries with intact traditions and stable socio-economic systems may in fact be very heterogeneous in ethnicity. The obvious solution is to obtain matched samples from the cultures studied. However, when matching for one variable that very psychometric control often causes mismatching on other salient factors. For example, being Black in South Africa does not mean the same as being Black in London since these matched samples may differ on variety of socio-economic variables and matching for race would not produce equivalence.

The sample selected represents a larger population. To ensure that outcome researchers have in the past examined issues related to appropriate sample selection. Probably in most cases samples are chosen for convenience, typically by the availability of university students in many societies. Convenience sampling has often been criticized as being unrepresentative of the population for the obvious reasons of the higher level of education and socio-economic standing of university students (Wintre, North, & Sugar, 2001). However, whether university samples are useful in comparative research is really an empirical issue to be investigated by comparing university students and representative samples (Ellsworth & Gonzales, 2003) and not dismissed without evidence. Pernice, Van der Veer, Ommundsen and Larsen (2008) demonstrated that university students could be successfully utilized in both concept development and scale construction in an attitude toward immigrants study in New Zealand. Students in this study based their attitudes on the same criteria as the general population supporting the effect of shared cultural and political systems in both student and population samples.

Another type of sampling is called systematic since samples are selected based on some theory. Perhaps the objective is to study the effect of membership in religious organizations, and samples are drawn with proper controls from particular religious groups in different cultures. Another study may investigate the treatment of homosexuals in different cultures and select accordingly. The underlying theory might be the effect of religious dogmatism as related to tolerance.

In random sampling an effort is made to obtain representative sampling of the population studied. Random sampling is representative, and the results obtained are assumed to represent the population studied with little error. In random samples each individual has an equal and independent chance of being selected, and if the sample size is large enough the results are reliable and the population characteristics are represented with relatively little error (Offermann & Hellman, 1997). In general the larger the number of participants the less the sample will vary from the population characteristics (Heiman, 1996). The ideal in cross-cultural sampling is to utilize the random selection of participants. As noted that is often difficult or impossible, and convenience samples are frequently used. Although convenience sampling may not produce bias in the development of assessment instruments, the researcher must be cautious in generalizing the results of the study to the overall population of the culture.

Several sampling decisions have to be made when comparing cross-cultural groups. The primary decision is what cultural groups should be compared. That conclusion might in turn be based on some theory that predicts differences on the variables of interest. Secondly, all cultures have subsets of groups that vary on important dimensions. Therefore a second consideration is what sub groups should be included. Finally, the issue of how to select individual respondents must be considered.

Finally, in cross-cultural research the interest is not just to achieve representative samples, but also in ensuring equivalent samples. In practice this requires control for equivalence on demographic factors including socioeconomic status, occupation, religion or ideology, age and sex. For example, it would not be useful to compare a university sample from the United States with a sample drawn from Aboriginal fringe dwellers in Australia, since among many differences there would be obviously confounding educational and socio-economic effects. Demographic factors must therefore be controlled when comparing across cultures. However, even controlling for demographic variables may not provide proper comparative controls since, for example, being old in Japan or Europe may be very different experiences.

What an ambitious goal to attain information from all parts of the world about human nature and cultural practices! We learn that we are unique, yet similarly human. Cross-cultural researchers have a large task at hand, yet many work tirelessly to bring us valuable insight that allows us to gain a deeper understanding of human thought and behavior. At the end of this chapter, most readers are surprised at just what it takes to plan and execute a successful research study, especially when dealing with different cultures. Time and cost of travel, languages, government systems, (as in the story at the beginning of this chapter) belief systems, individualistic and collectivistic cultures are among just a few of the many factors to consider before doing a study. As we have read, a researcher needs to carefully consider every aspect of a research study to avoid possible errors that lead to inaccurate conclusions.

. . . .

WHAT DOES THIS MEAN TO ME?

Do you have an ethnocentric perspective when coming into contact with others from different backgrounds? Do you often think of the way you do things as the "right" way and others' behaviors as "wrong?" How many studies have you seen (particularly those circulating in social media) that you have just accepted as truth? Who did the study and why? How was the study done? Are the assessments based on solid evidence? Take notice of how you respond to new information, and then make necessary adjustments to be one step closer to multi-cultural competence in your everyday life.

. . . .

Chapter 3

Enculturation and Socialization

Man is born a barbarian, and only raises himself above the beast by culture.
—Baltasar Gracian (1601–1658)

Figure 3.1

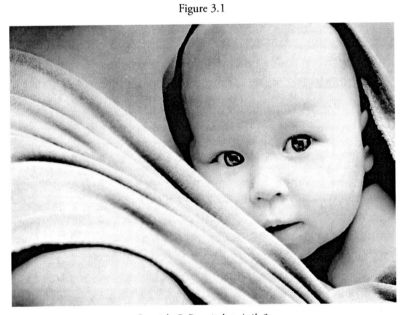

Copyright © Depositphotos/saiko3p.

In order to understand the nature of others around the world, we must pause and consider our own thoughts and behaviors and what makes us who we are. Understanding ourselves allows us to better understand others. The way we behave on a daily basis is heavily influenced by our own culture. Even from the day we are born, we are taught how to follow cultural rules. Most people feel a great need to fit into their surroundings because failure to do this may result in a difficult and complicated life experience. Without culture to mold us, we may not even have any resemblance at all to basic human behavior (Krum Krumov and Knud S. Larsen 2013). The way we behave is so engrained in us that it becomes second nature.

We don't think about our reactions in everyday life because it's natural and immediate. For this reason, it's a challenge to understand cultural practices that differ from our own.

The parents are a child's main socializing agents. We learn to adapt to our cultural norms from infancy through adulthood. During that time, we are sure to make mistakes but are constantly socialized by those around us. **Socialization** is the process by which we learn and internalize the rules and patterns of the society in which we live. This cultural learning affects our attitudes, values, and belief systems. There are four main socializing agents for a child: *parents, family, peers,* and *institutions.*

Enculturation is the *product* of the socialization process and is the subjective, underlying psychological aspects of culture that becomes internalized through development. After we are socialized, we become enculturated. Matsumoto points out that it's important to consider the economic conditions under which child-rearing takes place. Although there may be cultural ideas and attitudes about how a child should be raised, the most important aspect of parenting is to meet the basic needs necessary for a child to survive. Once basic needs are met, parents can focus on other goals such as instilling cultural values important to that culture. "Parenting goals provide the motivation and framework for what parents think is the best way to raise their children" (Mastumoto and Juang 2013).

TRADITIONAL CULTURES

A cross-cultural researcher will see that most cultures can be separated into two categories: traditional vs. untraditional. A **traditional culture** is based on the traditions, rules, and patterns of living that have been set by past generations. The untraditional (or modern) culture is constantly shifting and changing with new ideas and principles that are usually based on science and technological developments. The traditional culture is very slow to change or intolerant to change at all. Traditional cultures usually ascribe social roles to individuals, with emphasis placed on custom and routine, and there is a strong distinction between what is good or evil. Truth is established and does not change, and personal choices are restricted to what is deemed as appropriate social behavior. In nontraditional cultures, social roles are achieved by the individual, and personal freedom of choice is valued. What is good and evil can have very blurred lines. Truth comes from critical thinking and debate, and there is more tolerance for social practices such as homosexuality and premarital relationships. (Shiraev and Levy 2013).

Some individuals take comfort in knowing exactly whom they are supposed to be and how they are supposed to behave. The way that we are enculturated as discussed previously, is the lifestyle that we know and the way most of us feel comfortable. There comes a sense of safety and security in "following the rules" and being accepted by your group. Others however, may see a traditional culture as being a human constraint; they may be unable to live an individual life with no room for personal, emotional, or psychological growth. Having knowledge of one's culture and whether it is traditional or nontraditional can instantly foster more understanding and tolerance as we interact with others.

Traditions are the guideposts driven in our subconscious minds. The most powerful ones are those we can't even describe, aren't even aware of.

—Ellen Goodman

HUMAN DEVELOPMENT

Human development is an important part of understanding Cultural Psychology. Nature vs. Nurture is an enduring issue in Psychology and continues to be a question as more cross-cultural studies are evaluated. **Human development** is viewed as the changes in physical, psychological, and social behavior that are experienced by individuals across the life span, from conception to death. Human development isn't always growth but also decline and modification as one is socialized into a particular culture (Shiraev and Levy 2013). Cultural differences can be noted at every stage of life throughout the world.

PRENATAL PERIOD

This excerpt from *Cross-Cultural Psychology* (2013) explains that even before birth, there may be substantial differences between cultures.

Reading 3.1

In London and Beijing, as well as in any other part old the planet, the **prenatal period**—typical time between conception and birth—is 38 weeks. From the beginning, the developing embryo in a mother's womb can be exposed to either favorable or unfavorable conditions. For instance, the natural environment around the mother could be stable or unstable, safe or dangerous. Across the world, environmental problems and perilous conditions, such as hunger, violence, excessive radiation, exposure to chemicals, and air and water pollution, to name a few, can cause various complications in pregnancy and serious birth defects. The availability or lack of professional prenatal care is also a crucial factor affecting the unborn child's development. There are many common cognitive and behavioral trends related to pregnancy. Studies show, for instance, that in most countries, when a family expects a child, boys are desired more than girls (Hortacsu et al., 2001), and cross-nationally, teen pregnancies are more common in rural than in urban populations (Barber, 2001).

The fetus's life can be interrupted by a mother's decision to terminate her pregnancy. Nearly 50 million abortions are performed in the world each year. Almost 60 percent of them take place in developing countries, where close to 90 percent of the over 20 million illegal and unsafe abortions are performed each year. This is despite the fact that in many cases abortion in developing countries is restricted by law and condemned by religion. The risk of death from an unsafe, or illegal, abortion in a developing country is many times higher than the risk in developed countries. An estimated 21.6 million unsafe abortions took place worldwide in 2008, almost all in developing countries. Numbers of unsafe abortions remain relatively stable in the past decade: there are about 14 unsafe abortions per 1,000 women aged 15–44 years (WHO, 2011). Countries vary in terms of frequency of abortions performed.

Attitudes toward pregnancy also differ. In traditional collectivist countries, such as Malaysia, Singapore, Indonesia, Philippines, and Thailand, pregnancy is more family centered with active participation and guidance from family (Gardiner et al., 1998). In individualist societies, childbirth tends to be a rather private affair. However, one should be careful and try not to make stereotypical judgments. Many foreign exchange students, for example, mentioned to us how open many Americans are about their pregnancies: People make official statements, inform relatives and friends, and throw parties to spread the word about their condition. However, in many countries, such as Russia, pregnancy is commonly kept secret until the changes in the woman's body become obvious. Husbands are not only absent when their wives give birth but are also prohibited from entering birth clinics and may be escorted out by the police if they dare to enter the facility. Tradition and law often go hand in hand.

In addition, Shiraev and Levy mention several different customs from immigrant women in a maternity ward in the United States. For example, Russian mothers believe a child is not supposed to be seen by strangers for at least one month so that he or she is protected from the "evil eye." It can be bad luck to the child. Vietnamese mothers don't want to be exposed to cold because it disrupts the equilibrium that is believed to be crucial to good health. Muslim mothers are to be examined, and the baby delivered by female health workers only.

CHILDHOOD

Childhood is a dynamic period of life in any society. One similarity found in every culture is the wish to emerge from childhood as a competent and productive adult (Matsumoto 2013). What makes one "competent and productive" differs between cultures however. To function well in one society, you may be a skilled hunter and able to provide for others. In

Figure 3.2 Socialization begins at birth even with infant sleeping arrangements.

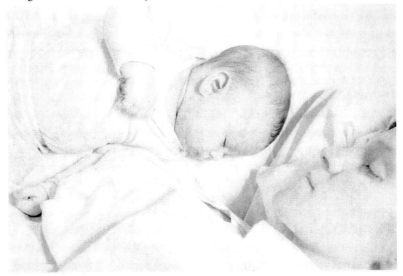

Copyright © Depositphotos/oksixx.

other places around the world, a productive individual will receive a high level of education. One thing is very clear: the child's parents, families, teachers, and peers have a large impact on the development of personality and behavior.

The way a child is socialized is dependent on multiple factors. Is it a collectivistic or individualistic culture? What about family values? In some cultures, the grandparents and extended family do much of the child-rearing. There are some individuals in Polynesian cultures that may bear a child to give to another family that is unable to have their own. In many cultures, the mother is never separated from the child but straps the child to her as she goes about her daily activities. Americans feel that holding a child too often can "spoil" the child. Attitudes about education, gender roles, and religious ideologies all play a role in a child's development and will influence thoughts and behaviors throughout an entire lifetime.

CO-SLEEPING

As soon as a child is born, attitudes and values about child-rearing are evident by something as simple as where a newborn baby sleeps. In the United States, it's very common to have an infant sleep close to you for a few weeks to a few months, but he or she is usually in another smaller bed such as a small crib or bassinet. Many cultures cannot understand this separation between mother and child. Upon learning the sleeping arrangements of many American children, some mothers in other cultures expressed concern for these infants.

Why do many American parents sleep separately from their newborn? There are several reasons for this. First, some pediatricians and other health-care professionals have suggested that co-sleeping can create an unhealthy dependence on parents. There is no evidence however, that sleeping alone has actually created independence or autonomy. (McKenna and McDade 2005). In addition, there were some safety

Figure 3.3 Mothers around the world may keep their baby with them at all times.

Copyright © Depositphotos/topten22photo.

concerns with parents unintentionally suffocating their newborn by sleeping too closely or rolling on top of the child. Because of our individualistic society, it makes sense for us to create independence at a young age. To have a child sleeping through the night in his or her own space is seen as a success, one step in the right direction to becoming an independent and successful adult. Understanding that a child may need some security and comfort while sleeping alone, American parents provide things such as "security blankets" or soft, plush animals or a pacifier to soothe him or her. Pacifiers or thumb sucking is frowned upon by mothers in some cultures.

Another factor that makes it easier to have a child sleep separately is having access to additional rooms within the same house. One of the most exciting things associated with parenthood in the U.S. and other developed countries is the ability to prepare a "nursery." In many cases, colors are chosen, a full-size crib is purchased, there may even be matching bedding and window treatments. Furniture such as dressers and changing tables are all common to a baby's new room. In many households around the world, the thought of having a separate room just for baby is unfathomable. Not only is it too costly but also separating the infant from the parents can create hardship on both parents and infants.

Parents in other parts of the world (especially in Eastern societies) feel quite the opposite about co-sleeping than do many Americans. They believe that keeping the infant close to you at all times, especially during the night, creates a stronger bond and instills more security and feelings of safety within a child. It's not uncommon to have a child sleep right next to the parents for years. When a new baby comes along, the child moves to a different part of the room or may sleep with another family member. In many households, entire families sleep together in one small room and may share one or two beds. In the name of family bonding and in some cases safety, everyone stays close to one another during the night and sometimes during the day too. It's important to point out that there may be variations even within the same culture. In America, depending on socio-economic conditions and ethnic backgrounds, sleeping independently and co-sleeping are both used even though traditionally we are an individualistic society that fosters independence by having the child in a separate sleeping space.

PARENTING

As stated earlier, parents are the single most important influence on a child and the socializing process. It's the parents' responsibility first, to make sure the basic needs for survival are met and second, to teach their child cultural values and norms. Baumrind (1971) identified three different types of global parenting patterns. They are *authoritarian, permissive,* and *authoritative.* Later, a fourth one was added called *uninvolved.*

Krum Krumov and Knud S. Larsen explain these parenting styles as well as cultural differences.

Reading 3.2

AUTHORITATIVE VERSUS AUTHORITARIAN CHILDREARING APPROACHES AND CULTURAL DIFFERENCES

Research on child rearing in the United States identified three styles of parenting (Baumrind, 1971). *Authoritative* parents provide the child with care that is firm, but also reasonable and fair. Control in authoritative child rearing is dependent on the child's maturity, and parents typically display warm and open affection for their children. Guidelines are provided by authoritative parents, but not rigidly enforced as children are given freedom to choose dependent on their level of development and responsibility. In the second style of parenting *authoritarian* parents demand obedience first and foremost and provide strict control over the child. Authoritarianism may have grown out of harsh environments where parents see their role as keeping their children out of harm's way. Baumrind's research also identified *permissiveness* as a parental style. Permissive parents allow their children to live their own lives without much interference or discipline. This style of parenting seems close to that of the uninvolved parents identified by Maccoby and Martin (1983). However, permissive parents are involved with their children and exhibit warmth in their relationships, whereas uninvolved parents are just indifferent.

The initial results from American studies supported the superiority of the authoritative style in many studies. Children who grow up with parents that use the authoritative childrearing style develop more useful traits including more positive emotions, more self-confidence and self-reliance (Karavasilis, Doyle, & Markiewicz, 2003). The authoritative parenting style prepares the child well for life resulting in children that are psychologically healthy and competent, and who live with fewer anxieties compared to children brought up by other parenting styles. By contrast children of authoritarian parents displayed more anxiety and develop cognitive styles that lack spontaneity and curiosity. The benefits for children of authoritative parents are not just confined to childhood. Studies of adolescents produced similar positive results. Adolescents with authoritative parents are more socially adept, tend to have higher self-esteem and display more creativity (Collins & Laursen, 2004; Spera, 2005). The authoritative style of parenting seems to have a positive effect on the child's sense of optimism and helps create the belief that the child lives in a well-ordered world with developmental goals that are attainable. These effects are carried over into university life where students from authoritative homes displayed less depression and greater social adaptability (Jackson, Pratt, Hunsberger, & Pancer, 2005).

For comparative psychology an important question is whether these styles are manifested in other cultures than the United States, or to what degree are they culturally specific? Are the positive outcomes of authoritative parents limited to children living in the United States? Chao (2001) argued that it is important to understand the dominant cultural values before investigating parental styles. The efficacy of parental styles may well depend on underlying values to which the child must conform. Chao argued that the role of training in Chinese culture is unique and not covered by the Baumrind's parental styles. However, in another study in China authoritarian parenting was related negatively to school adjustment, whereas children from authoritative homes fared better in overall social adjustment (Chen, Dong, & Zhou, 1997). In a multicultural society like the U.S. perhaps the efficacy of authoritative approaches to childrearing depends on the child's ethnic or cultural group? However, a review of more recent studies confirms the continuous advantage of authoritative approaches to childrearing that are independent of the larger cultural values associated with collectivistic or individualistic cultures (Sorkhabi, 2005). Parental warmth and acceptance of the child are important factors in positive outcomes everywhere, and authoritative parenting takes on universal value as the advantages are not limited by culture. Comparative studies have largely confirmed the advantages of authoritative versus authoritarian parenting as it produces more solidarity in families and better mental functioning (Dwairy, Achoui, Abouserie, & Farah, 2006).

Parenting philosophies tend to change over time. This is certainly the case in the United States. Older generations tell of a time when there were mostly authoritarian parents and a child didn't dare disobey for fear of corporal punishment. Many older people quickly add how they "learned to respect" their elders! Their experiences weren't always painted in a bad light. Teachers had a right to discipline students, even physically. The biblical reference of "spare the rod, spoil the child" was not uncommon in many cultures. Children were to be seen and not heard.

WHAT DOES THIS MEAN TO ME?

What type of parenting style did your parents use? How did family cultural values affect the parenting style used? How did this type of parenting affect who you are? Should you choose to have children, would you use this same parenting style and why? Did your parents use the same parenting style that their parents used with them? How can understanding parenting styles and how one was raised be beneficial in your life?

As research showing negative consequences of harsher parenting has gained momentum, and human rights (for every age) have become more salient, parent-child relationships in many ways, have been redefined in America. We have a tendency to believe that we are becoming better parents through most of these changes and that our children are being better protected and cared for unlike generations past. We don't allow our children to go wherever they want at young ages or do dangerous things like climb tall trees or use knives. We even have prearranged play dates where children (along with the parents) play in a supervised and safe environment! But have American parents got it all backwards? Some would say this is definitely the case.

Please read the following article by Christine Gross-Loh, who had the opportunity through her traveling to experience parenting and child-rearing practices around the world.

http://www.huffingtonpost.com/christine-grossloh/have-american-parents-got-it-all-backwards_b_3202328.html

Some students who read this article would not be willing to allow for certain activities mentioned. Are the topics discussed in this article right or wrong? Are they good or bad for a child? We can see how our upbringing and culture set our minds on how things should be as a child and as a parent. This is a mind-set that is very hard to change. Did your own opinion on parenting change as you read the article?

SIBLINGS AND EXTENDED FAMILY

Siblings will spend just as much time, if not more time, with a child as do the parents in many cultures. Krumov et al. discuss this in the following excerpt.

Reading 3.3

RELATIONSHIPS WITH SIBLINGS

Our relationships with brothers and/or sisters play important roles in socialization. In large families older siblings may be delegated roles as caregivers (Weisner & Gallimore, 1977). When children are close in age siblings are present along with parents for the most important events of a child's life. *The significance of family and cultural life is filtered through the eyes of siblings who struggle with similar family and cultural values.* Cultural values including interdependence are taught via sibling relationships. Our social assessment of right and wrong develop in sibling relationships whether cultivating aggression or empathy (Parke, 2004). As time moves on appropriate sex role behavior and gender relationships are learned primarily from siblings. Of all the influences in life the role of siblings is likely to be the most enduring as parents typically pass from the scene, but relationships with brothers and sisters are sustained until the end. However, the main focus of research has been on the child-parent relationship and we have only modest information on what must be the very significant influence of siblings (McHale, Crouter, & Whiteman, 2003).

Extended family, such as grandparents, aunts, uncles, and cousins, especially in collectivistic cultures, can play a major role in a child's development. "It takes a village to raise a child" is a common expression still used today, that refers to anyone who can influence and care for one individual child. There are teachers, religious leaders, school administrators, club leaders, coaches, and even the parents of close friends who can all influence a young person's life. Parents work together with other adults in the community to teach a youngster how to behave and interact within his or her culture. It is not uncommon for the parents, grandparents, and married siblings to all live under one roof in various parts of the world. They share resources, support each other, and can share the everyday work load. In China for example, grandparents will raise a child while the parents go to work and provide for the family financially. It makes perfect sense that the older generation cares for the young because they are respected, and it is believed that they have the wisdom to teach valuable lessons to their grandchildren.

It's quite different here in the United States. Although multigenerational families living together are on the rise, it's still seen as a less desirable living arrangement compared to dwelling with just the nuclear family. Furthermore, the idea for grandparents to live with and care for their grandchildren just isn't as accepted as it may be in other cultures. In America, it may be a sign of poor economics, a burden on grandparents, or parents who are lacking in their duty to rear their own offspring (Matsumoto and Juang 2013). Some foreigners who come to America are shocked at what they see as a lack of respect and underutilization of our older family members. In more traditional cultures, the wisdom of older members is valued and their advice welcomed. In many cases, it's through the grandparents and elders of a group that valuable information is passed to the younger generations.

INSTITUTIONS

What is being learned at home from siblings, parents, and extended family is being reinforced through schools, churches, and any other group in which a child may participate. Institutions will continue to socialize cultural values and rules. In some Asian cultures, for example, children are taught from a very young age about the importance of recycling, and these schools spend more time than most American schools teaching this concept. The Mofu tribe in Northern Cameroon for example, may spend more time teaching the children what is relevant in their everyday life such as how the harvests are reliant on rainfall and when and how the crops will be successful. They may learn more about nature because they are living very closely to it. In many parts of the world, eating bugs is a normal part of the diet, and children must learn what creatures are dangerous or toxic. They may even have class outdoors and gain a first-hand knowledge of their environment and how it affects them. What is specifically important to their lives and how one should learn and behave in their own environment are the key principles in a

Figure 3.4 Peers have a large impact on how we learn cultural attitudes and behaviors.

Copyright © Depositphotos/Sam741002.

child's education within a culture.

ADOLESCENCE

The adolescent years in life can vary greatly between cultures. Industrialized countries typically have this stage of life fitting nicely between childhood and adulthood and is viewed as an important process in personal identity development. Cultural conditions determine whether this is even considered a developmental stage at all. Consider girls as young as 12 who are immediately thrust into adulthood as they are married and begin living with their husband's family. They don't have the teen years that many American students have that include hanging out with friends, learning to drive, dating, and being involved in various clubs. In some places like Cambodia, when a girl turns 13, she is given the opportunity to live in her own space that is usually separate from the family home and is encouraged to explore her sexuality by having any male visitors she prefers. In America, this practice would be considered by many to be child abuse and would probably create quite an uproar. Is a 13-year-old girl old enough to make adult decisions? The answer to this question may vary greatly between cultures.

Some teenagers are living in the adult world because of the educational systems. By the time they are 15 or 16 years of age, they are out of school and out in the work force. Sexual activity and alcohol consumption begin at ages that are typically younger than teens in the U.S. Due to economic hardship or war-torn environments, some youth around the world acquire adult roles by needing to help with household finances, caring for everyday household activities, or even being recruited by militia to fight. Certainly these teens don't experience the type of developmental stage that so many cultures feel is crucial to personal development.

PEER CULTURES

It's during adolescence that a child may look more to influences outside of family about what is appropriate behavior within the culture. Parents may not be as current on cultural shifts, and in order to fit in, a teen may need to rely more on peers for information. It's important to note that while these years are important to youth in so many cultures, not ALL young people have exposure to peer groups. Nontraditional types of education or rural settings can limit any interaction and therefore, socialization from peers. Some believe that socialization may actually inhibit personal development and is viewed as detrimental to self-actualization. Those who disagree believe that peer socialization is a crucial step in learning about yourself by learning to get along with others.

Margaret Mead (1978) identified three types of peer cultures with varying levels of peer influence on the socialization process. There are *post-figurative cultures, co-figurative cultures,* and *pre-figurative cultures.* In a **post-figurative** culture, the change is slow and the socialization process is typically done by elders in the village who share their knowledge and ideas with the younger generations. Parents, grandparents, and teachers share their wisdom on how to become a successful and competent adult. In a **co-figurative** culture, peers begin to play a larger role in the socialization process. Change is happening more rapidly, but parents still have an important role in teaching their child. Peers in this culture tend to turn to each other for advice and information. In a **pre-figurative** culture, change is so rapid that many adults are turning to the younger generation for knowledge because the information they have may not be sufficient for the needs of the child. What type of peer culture do you feel we have in America, and do you believe this has changed within the last 100 years?

While human development and the enculturation process in no way stops at the teen years, our enculturation has been strongly absorbed by young adulthood. We are so deeply entrenched in our own way of life that it's very difficult to change, which in turn makes it a challenge to adjust to differences when visiting or living in another culture. The more aware we are of our own attitudes, beliefs, and traditions influenced by our own culture, the more we understand the depth of another's cultural behaviors. It's important to research differences before we travel or live abroad or if we are associating with someone from another culture. Research may alleviate misunderstandings and frustrations when coming in contact with a different cultural background.

Chapter 4

Critical Thinking

"Children must be taught how to think, not what to think."

—Margaret Mead

Figure 4.1

Copyright © Depositphotos/Kentoh.

Reading 4.1

This story could have been told in New Orleans. Or maybe in New York. Or perhaps in Tokyo, Cape Town, or Buenos Aires. A woman walks into a doctor's office complaining that she's a zombie. The doctor, trying his best to convince her otherwise, says, "You're walking and talking, aren't you?"

"Zombies walk and talk," replies the patient.

"Well, you're breathing, too."

"Yes, but zombies breathe."

"Okay, what *don't* zombies do? Do they bleed?"

"No, *of course not*," says the patient.

The doctor replies, "Good. Then I'm going to stick this needle into your arm and we'll see if your idea is right or wrong."

So he plunges the needle deep into the woman's arm, and, sure enough, blood starts to pour out of the wound. The woman is aghast. In utter dismay, she turns to the doctor and says, "My God, I was wrong…. Zombies *do* bleed."

What is the moral of this story? Compelling facts are quite often not compelling enough. What matters more is our interpretation of these facts. One of the most significant characteristics of our thinking is the way in which we become personally invested in—and then tightly cling to—our beliefs and interpretations. This tendency, called the belief perseverance effect, can frequently lead us to freely distort, minimize, or even ignore any facts that run contrary to our reality.

The woman in the previous story was not going to let anything prevent her from believing she was a zombie, no matter what evidence may have proved her wrong. This *belief perseverance* she was exhibiting is not uncommon to our human thinking. We find great difficulty in changing our thinking patterns, even if there's strong evidence to suggest that our thoughts are wrong. Our beliefs and perceptions are so strong that they can be a tremendous barrier to understanding and accepting cultural differences. **Critical thinking** is an active and systematic cognitive strategy to examine, evaluate, and understand events, solve problems, and make decisions on the basis of sound reasoning and valued evidence. Also, to be a critical thinker we need to maintain an attitude that is both open minded and skeptical, recognizing the distinction between facts and theories (Shiraev and Levy 2013).

We have all developed our own **schema,** which is a structure in our minds that houses and organizes our knowledge, beliefs, attitudes, and perceptions based on our past experiences. We immediately and automatically categorize everything that we face in our environment, including people, places, events, concepts, memories, and feelings. (Shiraev and Levy 2013). The way a schema is developed and used has to do with the way we learn and process the astronomical amount of stimuli that we come in contact with every day. If we didn't categorize, we would be overwhelmed with too much information. Our schema provides a framework for us to understand any new information we encounter. Evolutionary psychologists would tell us that one of the reasons our cognitive structure (or schemata) that organizes all of this outer stimuli is wired into us is for survival purposes. Am I safe? That looks like a lion, and I'm categorizing that into the file titled "dangerous animal who may want to eat me, I need to act!" Of course we do all of this processing without even realizing it. We don't have to think too deeply; it's as if our mind is on auto-pilot.

"Two thirds of what we see is behind our eyes."

—Chinese proverb

ERRORS IN THOUGHT PROCESSES

When faced with new information, we immediately compare the contents to see if it may fit into our existing schema. We attempt to understand and process our world by organizing information in this manner. This process is not unlike a "shortcut" which may be more efficient but can lend itself to inaccuracies. In order to be aware of the way we process information, we need to stop and think about our thoughts! It may be difficult to do at first, but being aware of what we are thinking and what comes naturally to us as we are given new information is one of the first steps to becoming a critical thinker. **Meta-thinking** is when we think about the *way* we think and the way in which we categorize things in our environment. To have a "meta-thought" is to think about and analyze our own thoughts!

Figure 4.2 We often believe, "My way is right, your way is wrong" no matter what the circumstances.

Copyright © Depositphotos/stuartmiles.

When we have a schema that structures our thoughts and perspectives of our world, we have a tendency to believe that what we already know and understand is the "right" way of thinking, and thoughts and behaviors that differ from our own are "wrong." In other words, what's familiar to us is equivalent to being "good," and what is new and unknown is considered "bad" or inappropriate. This is something with which we ought to be aware because our way is not necessarily better or worse than the way others do things.

BIASES AND STEREOTYPES

What does it mean to have a *"bias?"* A **Bias** is when we rely on vivid but not necessarily accurate information about the world around us. Our schemas can bias our perceptions of reality to make them consistent with what we already believe. When we view the world with what Shiraev and Levy (2017) call our "Schema colored glasses," we see outer stimuli with varying degrees of distortion and misrepresentation. All of us have what may be called an "unconscious bias." We don't even realize that we view things in a particular way and are certainly not aware that our perception of things may be incorrect.

Please watch the following video that may open our eyes to just how biased we may be.

https://www.ted.com/talks/yassmin_abdel_magied_what_does_my_
headscarf_mean_to_you?language=en

We should never underestimate how strongly our prior beliefs, knowledge, and expectancies (schemata) can affect our current experiences, impressions, and perceptions (Shiraev and Levy 2017).

A **stereotype** (which will also be discussed in a later chapter) is when we assume that all members of a group have the same characteristics. A stereotype can be positive or negative. We may not even be aware that we have a stereotype. We put others in a category without even thinking about it. Gender stereotypes are still very strong as you could see from the previous video. Here are some other examples of stereotypes we many have:

- All African American males who are tall are good at basketball or are involved in some type of athletics;

- Mexican immigrants are all criminals and want to drain American resources;

- Asian students are all smart and make the top grades; and

- All citizens living in Africa are poor and unhappy and just trying to survive.

There are many other examples. It's not wrong to recognize that there are many similarities within groups of people that are based on their culture. When we automatically expect however, that every member is the same, we deny them his or her own unique personality and individual practices. Each individual should be treated without preconceived ideas of how he or she should act or behave.

PREJUDICE AND DISCRIMINATION

Many use the terms "prejudice" and "discrimination" interchangeably. There is a simple difference between the two. A **prejudice** is an unfair, intolerant attitude of an individual or group of people. This may include negative statements made to people in our own circles, frustration when an immigrant receives medical care or a job in the community, or energy spent trying to make others aware of perceived injustices by individuals or groups of people from another culture or ethnicity. **Discrimination** is a negative action against a person or group of people based on cultural or ethnic differences. This may include not offering someone a job, not renting someone property, or verbally assaulting someone from another country or culture. Unfortunately, discriminatory acts can be more serious when intolerance leads to physical harm or damaging property based on these differences.

Many times these attitudes are passed from generation to generation. Most of the intolerance toward differences have been taught by parents and grandparents. Children may accept as truth, the perceived characteristics and negative intentions of those who come from other places. The goal would be then, to become a critical thinker and not just accept the negative ideas and perceptions of others that are usually riddled with flawed thinking about those from differing backgrounds. We should value every individual and his or her background. The video included in this chapter called *The Danger of a Single Story* discusses how we can change our mindset to combat our biased thinking and prejudices toward others.

USE OF WORDS AND PHRASES

Let's take a moment to practice some meta-thinking and ask ourselves if we might be guilty of inaccurate thoughts when processing new information. The very words we use to describe others can have a bias even if it's unintended. For example, if we are trying to describe someone, which words would we choose to use: daring or reckless, innocent or naïve, old or mature? We can agree that in most languages, several words can have the same basic meaning but have a slightly different attitude or "feel" to it. If we want to paint someone in a positive light, we would choose words that possess a more positive facet. The words we use may imply another underlying meaning whether it be positive or negative. Being mindful of the words used to describe another situation or person is a good start to analyzing our thinking in general, which is one step closer to becoming multi-culturally competent.

DICHOTOMOUS AND CONTINUOUS VARIABLES

Shiraev and Levy (2013) point out that we tend to categorize others or groups of others in an ALL or NOTHING category. We tend to make statements like "He is crazy" or "Those people are all introverted." There are very few instances where something is either in one category or another. Is someone really "crazy?" or was there an instance that he may have behaved in a way that you felt was inappropriate? A few examples of phenomena that may be put into two mutually exclusive categories is when something is turned on or off, someone is dead or alive (even this can be argued, at times), or a woman is pregnant or not pregnant. **Dichotomous variables** are those things that fit into either one group or another with nothing in between. Can you think of any other examples? It might be a bit challenging as there just aren't many that fit into this category.

We've mentioned individualism vs. collectivism in relation to culture. Does this mean that every person who lives in this culture follows this lifestyle? Can one family lean more toward individualism than collectivism? The answer is most definitely yes! We need to account for individual differences. There are varying degrees or shades of gray with almost everything we encounter in our experiences, and these degrees are referred to as **continuous variables** (Shiraev and Levy 2013). Once we accept that people or situations in life may lie on a continuum and avoid thinking in terms or all or nothing, it aids us in seeing others more in depth, with all of their complexities and unique personalities that simply cannot be placed in a particular category. Shiraev and Levy (2017) identify some dichotomous and continuous variables. Of the following, what may be considered a dichotomous relationship, and what can lie along a continuum or degrees?

On–Off
Racist–Nonracist
Present–Absent
Liberal–Conservative

Married–Single
Perfect–Imperfect
Licensed–Unlicensed
Feminine–Masculine

---

*Everyone and anyone is much more simply human than otherwise,
more like everyone else than different.*

—Harry Staci Sullivan (1892–1949), American Psychiatrist

SIMILARITIES VS. DIFFERENCES

In the video clip from *Race: The Power of an Illusion*, we learned that just below the surface we are all basically the same. Why, then, do we tend to focus on these superficial differences? One group of people has straight hair and rounded faces, another group light hair and pale skin, or dark skin and curly hair. Differences such as these tend to have a deeper meaning to so many around the world. We have so much in common just by being a part of the human race. We can find similarities as well as differences in just about anything we encounter. We must keep in mind that when comparing any two phenomena, such as infancy and old age, men and women, religion and science, it's important to know that there is always some common ground. If we would focus more on what we have in common instead of what makes us different, it will encourage a more tolerant and understanding perspective. Let's practice! Consider the following pairings of what appear to be two completely opposite categories. Can you find any similarities between them at all?

- God vs. Satan

- Individualism vs. Collectivism

- Infancy vs. Old Age

- Men vs. Women

- Religion vs. Science

In almost everything we encounter, we can find similarities between them. Even if at first, they may seem to be completely opposed.

OVERGENERALIZATION

You open a fortune cookie and find that the words written on that small piece of paper are perfectly applicable to you! What great "fortune" to find these words that guide you, or at the very least, understand who you are. Why then, do most of us not completely embrace this idea or guidance? Because we understand that these words are written to apply to many different people. Other examples may include astrological forecasts, self-help books, and psychic readings, to name a few. They are generalized statements about human nature more often than not. We tend to describe people in generalities. How does this apply to cultural psychology? How often have we taken just a few facts that we may know about an individual or group of individuals and applied this information to an entire country or culture? How often do we have linear thinking without believing that there may be more possibilities than we first imagined? Statements that are overly inclusive of all humans are referred to as a **Barnum statement,** and our willingness to accept these statements as truth is called the **Barnum effect.** It's a "one size fits all" type of thinking (Shiraev and Levy 2013).

We should begin to analyze the way we categorize and think of others. Do we have just a single story? Are we guilty of applying just a few impressions of a small group or individual to an entire group? For example, what are our very first thoughts when we think of Africa; are they immediately turned to unclothed, starving children in mud huts or dirty hospitals and unbearable heat? Media and literature can play a large role in how we think about others around the globe. What information is being focused on in the news, what videos are shown again and again, and do we have the full story? Please watch the following video, and see if your perception changes based on her story.

https://www.ted.com/talks/chimamanda_adichie_the_danger_of_a_single_story?language=en

I would imagine that most Americans may be surprised to hear that there are loving, stable, and happy childhoods in Africa just as there are here. We need to discover the full story. We should not accept what we think we know about others as truth.

BELIEF PERSEVERANCE

We've learned the importance of getting all of the information, not jumping to conclusions about any person or situation, and the importance of understanding that each person is unique and complex. When we do receive new information that differs from our previous thoughts, what do we do with it? Do we mend our flawed thinking and decide that we will never misjudge again? Not likely. As humans, most of us have a tendency to want to hold on to what we know and believe even if we suspect it may not be completely accurate. We feel a sense of peace and security when our environment and experiences as we know them, remain the same. The expression "old habits die hard" is associated with this idea. Change can be very hard and so can admitting that our previous perceptions are inaccurate and should be shifted.

Figure 4.3 Can we assimilate new information, or are we stuck in a box?

Copyright © Depositphotos/honzahruby.

• •

WHAT DOES THIS MEAN TO ME?

Are you able to remember a time when you have unfairly judged someone else based exclusively on things you have heard? Did you base your entire assessment on just one experience? What is your automatic reaction when dealing with new information? Do you try to give others the benefit of the doubt, or do you automatically assume a character flaw based on a few encounters? Do you take into consideration one's ethnic/cultural background and how this may influence behavior? What are some things you might do to change your perspective when dealing with others? What are some ways that you can expand your schema and begin to "think outside the box?" Think of some concrete things that you can do to improve your critical thinking skills.

• •

The story at the beginning of this chapter highlights this phenomenon called **belief perseverance.** "Don't confuse me with the facts" is another mindset that one might take when given relevant, new information (Shiraev and Levy 2013). For some cultures, the idea of learning, growing, and changing based on scientific facts and studies is more acceptable than others. The more traditional cultures that don't focus on scientific conclusions will usually have a much harder time accepting any changes that affect daily life and especially religious ideologies. Sometimes, even in industrialized countries, no matter what the new scientific studies prove, we may refuse to believe them especially if it requires a change in thinking or behavior on our part. Why are we prone to be "stubborn" in our thinking? We should work on having the ability to keep an open mind and accept that there may be differences in what we value and believe is correct. At the very least, we can attempt to understand why others may have opposing views and varying behaviors.

INTERACTING WITH OTHERS

When it comes to initial impressions of others, it is human nature to make quick judgements. Evolutionary experts will say this is because of our innate ability to recognize a threat for survival. Our first impression of another tends to stick no matter what we observe later in the relationship. In addition, we tend to be quick to make negative assessments over positive ones. In social psychology, there's a researched finding about human interaction called the **actor/observer bias.** The way the actor (the one taking part in the behavior) and the observer (the one witnessing the behavior) explain the exact same behavior can differ. For example, if Tom (the actor) receives an A on an exam, he may believe this happened because he is a hard worker with great memory skills. Conversely, the observer may believe that Tom received an A because his parents spent time helping him do his homework and because he has more time during the day to study than most other students. Can you see that Tom attributed his own performance based on internal characteristics, and the observer attributed Tom's success to external factors? The observer believed he did well because he had more time to study and his parents were able to help him prepare, not because of any internal characteristics about natural ability.

FUNDAMENTAL ATTRIBUTION ERROR

Attribution theory is an important concept in social psychology. To what do we attribute the behaviors of others? Sadly enough, we tend to take credit for our own successes as something internal yet pin others' successes on things that are external to them (Bruya 2015). When we experience failure, we tend to deny that any internal characteristics were responsible and blame external causes. When others experience failure, we often attribute the behavior to internal causes. When behavior is attributed in this manner, it is called a **fundamental attribution error.** This is yet another form of flawed thinking that can have a negative impact on our interpersonal relationships as well as relationships between groups of people. We can improve this type of thinking and give those with whom we interact the benefit of the doubt rather than assuming the worst. As a whole, we lean toward attributing certain behaviors to entire groups of people based on possible misinformation and inaccurate observations of just a few.

SELF-FULFILLING PROPHECY

Sometimes, schemata can even help us create the behavior we expect from other people. In a classic study, pairs of participants played a competitive game (M. Synder and Swan 1978). The researchers told one member of each pair that his or her partner was either hostile or friendly. The player who was led to believe that his or her partner was hostile behaved differently toward that partner than did the player led to believe that his or her partner was friendly. In turn, those treated as hostile actually began to display hostility. When we bring about expected behavior in another person in this way, our impression becomes a **self-fulfilling prophecy** (Morris and Maisto 2016).

The way we treat others can have a significant influence on the way they behave even if it's not their common behavior. Can you see how this could become a hindrance to a child whose teacher believes is a "problem" child? The teacher (many times not even aware of it) will respond to this student and actually elicit the problem behavior. It can become a vicious cycle. How does this apply to cultural psychology? We may foster biases and stereotypes toward a group of people and consequently treat them in a way that encourages the very behavior we suspect. Then we may make mental notes that are something like, "See? Just as I suspected, I knew they would behave that way." We can work on eliminating any preconceived ideas of an individual or group of people to encourage fair judgment and consequently strengthen bonds between individuals and groups.

Being mindful of our own behaviors will allow us to see where we can improve and take the necessary actions to change. By becoming aware of our weaknesses in the way we think of or act toward others, we are taking a crucial step in improving our own relationships and on a larger level, between groups of people who have different cultural backgrounds and behaviors. Ultimately this can lead to a greater understanding and tolerance for differences around the world.

Chapter 5

Culture and Cognition

*We don't see things with our eyes; we see them through our eyes
and with our minds.*

—Anonymous

Figure 5.1

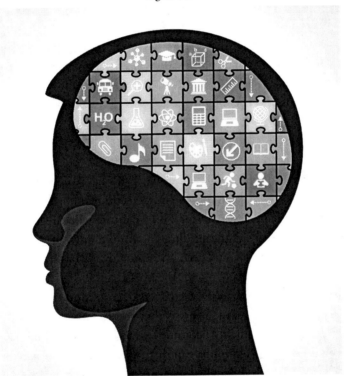

To fully understand cultural similarities and differences, we must look at basic processes of the mind. **Cognition** is conscious mental activity: the activities of thinking, understanding, learning, and remembering. All of the mental processes we use to transform sensory input into knowledge may differ based on our experiences and culture.

67

SENSATION AND PERCEPTION

As humans, we all experience **sensation** where the receptor cells are stimulated and sent to our brain to be processed. Should we assume that as humans we all experience these sensations in the same way? Do the differences in our physical environment, language, and everyday experiences create physical variation in brain function, or do these physiological aspects of our human nature remain constant in spite of cultural and behavioral variances?

When we watch Olympic swimmers, we may notice that they have a broad and muscular upper body. The width of their upper body may even surpass the lower portion which is small and lean. Now imagine the physique of a speed skater. Usually their thighs are large and muscular and may surpass in width their upper body. It's not surprising that their body will change based on these physical movements done repeatedly to gain strength in the area where they will need it the most. Swimmers need that upper body strength to pull themselves through the water; speed skaters will need that lower body strength to push themselves over the ice. Likewise, our brains can physically adapt to our daily needs and develop based on our daily activities. We all experience sensations, but the way these sensations are perceived can have significant differences. **Perception** is the way in which our sensations are processed and organized in our brain. We organize these sensations into meaningful patterns based on our experiences and environment.

LANGUAGE AND THE INFLUENCE ON SIGHT

The way we categorize stimuli in our mind, which we have learned from our earliest days, clearly has an influence on our sensations and perceptions. For example, are the colors we see the same as what someone else will see? Some cultures will categorize and describe colors differently which can cause a significant difference in the way our mind actually sees it. For example, in the English language we recognize roughly 11 basic colors. The Himba tribe in northern Namibia has 7 basic colors. They have certain shades of green and blue put together as one color. Because of this language categorization, tribe members have a hard time differentiating some blues and greens as they see them as the same color with a specific name. English speakers can quickly determine what is considered a blue color and what is considered green. However, the Himba can distinguish differences between shades of green that are so small in the minds of English speakers, that they are unable to see any difference at all. To the Himba people, these differences in green shades are very clear, as if they are different colors altogether. In their language, these shades of green are called by different names. It's important to realize that language and the way that we categorize our physical environment, may cause a literal change in the way our brains interpret the world.

Our language and environment have so much to do with the way we actually see the world. Our perceptions are different based on the way we are taught to view our world from a young age.

SOUND

In my classes, I play the theme song from *Jaws*, a movie released in 1975, which has had (and still has) a strong effect on many Americans who remember the film based on a shark that terrorized a small beach town. In fact, the idea of having a large fish attack at any moment kept many out of the water for a long time after the movie was released! In addition, the music associated with these attacks can still elicit fear even after so many years.

What was of particular interest to me after playing this sound clip, were my international students. I would ask them how the music made them feel and if it had any special meaning to them. If they were unfamiliar with the film (as most were), they weren't sure quite what to say about it. They said they liked the orchestra music and that it seemed to be building up to something. There were no feelings of anxiety or fear that other American students familiar with the movie said they felt. Their *perception* of this music was different based on their past experiences, or lack thereof, in this case.

The music we enjoy is most likely the music we have heard while growing up. We tie our memories and feelings to specific songs or types of music. When we are exposed to music from another culture, it can be hard to appreciate. Likewise, music that we love to listen to may be hard for others from different cultures to enjoy. The environment in which we are raised can make a difference in what types of sounds we like to hear. Did we grow up listening to the sounds of nearby birds or other animals, the sounds of the ocean crashing against the rocks, or the sounds of a city? Adjusting to the sounds from a different location, although it may seem like just a small change, can add to the stress of trying to adjust to a new culture.

TOUCH, SMELL, AND TASTE

How would it feel to walk barefoot in the dirt every day? Would we perceive it as soft and comfortable, or would we feel anxiety about getting dirty or receiving cuts and bruises? Many people in the Polynesian Islands (and many other places around the world) walk barefoot and build up callouses on their feet to the point that they don't even notice smaller things they step on. Fabrics that are customary and comfortable to wear in one culture may be found to be uncomfortable and undesirable in another. One of the basic emotions that we share globally is disgust. We can feel disgust if we believe we are touching something that is somehow contaminated. Would you touch a bug crawling around your feet? What about a snake, lizard, or rat? Many of us would shudder at the thought of it.

The following video is an example of how different our perceptions may be around the world.

https://www.youtube.com/watch?v=2OOs1l8Fajc

What were some of your natural reactions to this video and why? Would you be willing to live there for any amount of time?

Our sense of smell is very sensitive to new and different environments. While living a block from Chinatown in San Francisco, I was overwhelmed with the smell of food. The smell of all manner of seafood as well as many other foods that were unrecognizable, made my stomach churn. It was interesting to me that those who had lived there for years didn't even notice these odors. These people seem to be immune from the odors I perceived as offensive. We typically have the ability to adapt to new stimuli, and after some time, we don't even notice certain phenomena in our daily atmosphere. For example, we can see the end of our nose but do we even notice that anymore? Through sensory adaptation, we become very accustomed to sights, smells, sounds, taste, and even touch. **Sensory adaptation** is the tendency of our sensory system to respond LESS to stimuli that continues without change. Someone who visits you in a busy city who is from a rural atmosphere may be aware of a higher level of sound and may even be bothered by it. Conversely, if you visit this same friend in the country, you may have an "eerie" feeling at how quiet it is or experience feelings of boredom.

I have learned when talking to people from other cultures that for many, change in diet is one of the hardest aspects of adjusting to a new culture. Many have reported that they actually get sick from the food they eat and go to great lengths to find international markets where they can find food that is native to their home. Our body adjusts not only to outside stimuli but also to what it's used to on the *inside*. Would you be willing to eat juicy bugs for dinner? Imagine so many people around the world who love the added protein to round out a meal and may even see it as a delicacy. This diet of bugs, or any other type of animal, may conjure up gag reflexes for some. Shrimp is popular in America and doesn't seem to be much different than eating a bug except that it lives in water. We have to remove the slimy "gunk" off of the back, cook it till its gray appearance turns to a pinkish color, pull off the legs, crack and remove the exoskeletal shell, and pull off the tail before we pop it in our mouths. We are so used to this idea that most people have no problem with that at all. Depending on where you live, you may or may not be able to handle spicy foods. To eat something spicy when you're not used to it can not only be uncomfortable but can also cause sickness. Our cultural upbringing has a huge influence on what we perceive as disgusting or inviting in the way of food, sights, sounds, smells, and the overall "feel" of our environment.

INTELLIGENCE

In my research on cross-cultural intelligence and how it is defined, I was most impressed with the explanation given by Shiraev and Levy in their text *Cross-Cultural Psychology*. They discuss the original theories of intelligence, biological factors, and IQ scores, (and controversies regarding them) along with differences in test scores among cultures.

Reading 5.1

DEFINING INTELLIGENCE

First of all, what is **intelligence**? Ask psychology professors at your college or university. If you ask 10 of them, you will receive nine different definitions. Just nine? What about the tenth teacher? (If you are asking this question now you are already revealing curiosity, an important feature of your intelligence.) The tenth professor will simply refer you to the introductory psychology textbook currently in use.

A quick glance through several introductory psychology textbooks published in the 2000s would reveal that intelligence is defined in a variety of ways. For example, intelligence may be described as a set of mental abilities; the capacity to acquire and use knowledge; problem-solving skills and knowledge about the world; the ability to excel at a variety of tasks; or as a skill that allows us to understand, adapt, learn, reason, and overcome obstacles. Which point of view should we choose? First, most definitions include the word "knowledge." Intelligence is knowing and understanding the reality. Then, most definitions draw attention to problem solving, which leads to an assumption that intelligence is a set of mental skills that helps individuals to reach goals. Intelligence is also an ability to use knowledge and skills in order to overcome obstacles. And finally, intelligence helps in the adaptation to changing conditions.

Such an inclusive understanding of intelligence can be useful for cross-cultural psychologists because it allows them to incorporate the cultural factor in the discussion of intelligence. Indeed, people live in different environments and acquire knowledge and skills necessary to pursue goals and adapt to different cultural settings.

Intelligence is also inseparable from **cognition**, a diversified process by which the individual acquires and applies knowledge. It usually includes processes such as recognition, categorization, thinking, and memory.

There are several scientific approaches to intelligence. Let us consider them briefly, using the previous vignette as a starting point for discussion.

Some researchers, especially during the earlier stages of intelligence testing at the beginning of the twentieth century, suggested the existence of a general factor—or central cognitive function—that determines a certain level of performance on a variety of cognitive tasks (Spearman, 1927). The existence of this central cognitive function was evidenced by a set of positive correlations among performances on verbal, spatial, numerical, and other assessment problems. People with high academic ranking tended to score well on measures such as general knowledge, arithmetic ability, and vocabulary. On the contrary, people with low scores on verbal tasks were likely to have low scores on other tests. This approach inevitably encouraged the assumptions that some ethnic and racial groups are fundamentally different in their intellectual abilities.

Over the years, the idea of "one factor" that determines intellectual functioning has been frequently challenged. One such critic, Thurstone (1938), proposed the existence of not only one but rather three intellectual skills: verbal, mathematical, and spatial.

Sternberg (1985, 1997) also supported a hypothesis about a multidimensional structure of intelligence and suggested the existence of three fundamental aspects of intelligence: analytic, creative, and practical. According to his arguments, most intelligence tests measured only analytic skills. Analytic problems in the test are usually clearly defined, have a single correct answer, and come with all the information needed for a solution. On the contrary, practical problems are usually not clearly defined. The person has to seek additional information and offer various "correct" solutions to the problem under consideration. To solve these problems successfully, the person would need to have accumulated everyday experiences and be motivated enough to find the solution.

Studying the diversity of human behavior and achievement, Gardner (2007) argued that along with logical, linguistic, or spatial intelligence measured by psychometric tests, there are other special kinds of musical, bodily kinesthetic, and personal intelligence (a person's ability to understand himself or herself, or other people). However, as you may see, the ability to plan, evaluate a particular situation, and make useful decisions about the situation is essential for human survival and well-being. Then again, skills such as musical and body kinesthetic—in most cases—are not necessarily essential for human endurance and adaptation.

From the beginning of the empirical studies of intelligence, culture was claimed to be its important "contributor." For example, Piaget (1972) argued that intelligence has similar cross-cultural developmental mechanisms. On one hand, children in all countries assimilate new information into existing cognitive structures. On the other hand, these cognitive structures accommodate themselves to the changing environment. Vygotsky, a Russian psychologist (1978), believed that intelligence could not be understood without taking into consideration the cultural environment in which the person lives.

In psychology, most attention has been given to the so-called **psychometric approach to intelligence.** This view is based on an assumption that our intelligence can "receive" a numerical value (Wechsler, 1958). This approach is also probably the most controversial one because of an ongoing debate about how accurately these values can be assigned and interpreted.

From an introductory psychology class you perhaps remember that, typically, most intelligence tests contain a series of tasks. Each test contains several subtests that measure various cognitive skills. When you take the test, you are asked to solve verbal and nonverbal problems, make perceptual judgments, solve puzzles, find word associations, explain pictures in your own words, memorize sequences of words or numbers, and so on. After your answers are checked, your score is converted into a special score. Then your score is compared with the average score of your peers—presumably, and in most cases, this includes people of the same nationality and age group as you are. In fact, the comparison will yield your actual intelligence quotient, or for short, IQ. Approximately

95 percent of the population have scores on IQ tests within two standard deviations of 15. That means IQs of most people—95 out of 100—will be somewhere between 70 and 130.

There has long been intense controversy about the validity of measures and interpretation of intelligence test scores, and there are at least two major points in debates about intelligence testing:

1. What do intelligence tests actually measure?

2. How can it be proven that the test score was not influenced by factors such as the attitudes, motivation, or emotional states of test takers?

Critically important for those who attempt to interpret cultural differences on intelligence scores are (1) the distinction between cognitive potential, (2) cognitive skills developed through interaction with cultural environment, and (3) scores on a particular test. The problem is that the standard tests may not provide for the direct assessment of cognitive skills shaped by a particular cultural environment. Unless intelligence tests accommodate the activities that people perform in their day-to-day life, the tests created in one culture will continue to be biased against other cultural groups. This means that the test performance may not represent the individual's cognitive potential (Vernon, 1969). Moreover, factors such as language, test content, and motivation reportedly contribute to an individual's performance on tests (Sternberg, 2007). For example, there are many aspects of human intelligence, such as wisdom and creativity, that many tests are simply not designed to measure.

Another major point of most discussions is how to interpret the numerical value of intelligence. If 12-year-old boys and girls from a northern part of a city scored 90 on a test, whereas those from a southern part scored 105 on the same test, what does this mean? The most fired debates take place when intelligence value is assigned to ethnic or national groups. Apparently, some significant differences among people in body size, shape, and skin color do not evoke such heated discussions, and, as a result, emotions often overshadow a fair discussion of group differences between intelligence scores.

Before we continue our analysis, let us express one concern. As we just suggested, few issues in psychology have become as divisive as the concept of intelligence. Around the world the debates about intelligence are often motivated by a variety of political, ideological, and group interests (Helms, 2006). In some cases, a particular political agenda comes first and psychology serves as a provider of data. Scientific arguments are often put aside. We accept, of course, that people who want to advance their particular views could use psychology for this purpose. Therefore, the goals of cross-cultural psychology perhaps will be better served if these views are not rejected outright but are critically analyzed.

ETHNIC DIFFERENCES IN IQ SCORES

Most of the questions that cross-cultural psychology attempts to address are concerned with a set of measurable similarities and differences among different cultural, ethnic, and national groups. Are ethnic groups characterized by a particular pattern of intellectual ability? For example, can one prove that Italians, in general, are more creative than Germans, but that the German mode of thinking is more "precise" than the Brazilian mode? Do some cultural groups have a "better" memory than others? Do poverty and other devastating social problems influence intelligence? Is systematic formal schooling the key to human intellectual equality? Is such equality achievable in principle?

In the United States, early attempts to measure IQs began more than 100 years ago. These studies examined schoolchildren, army recruits, and immigrants arriving in this country. For example, in 1921, the National Academy of Sciences published the results of one of the first massive national studies on intelligence. The results allowed the organizers of this study to rank newly arrived immigrants according to their IQ scores. This is how the "intellectual" order of the immigrants looked: England, Holland, Denmark, Scotland, Germany, Canada, Belgium, Norway, Austria, Ireland, Turkey, Greece, Russia, Italy, and Poland. In addition, the data showed the first evidence that blacks generally scored lower than whites on those tests. It was also reported that the Polish in this study did not score significantly higher than the blacks did (Kamin, 1976).

Today various tests show differences in intelligence scores among large cultural groups. For example, in the United States, Asian Americans (of East Asian origins) score the highest, followed by European Americans, Hispanics, and lastly African Americans. Thus, on the average, African American schoolchildren score 10–15 percent lower on a standardized intelligence test than white schoolchildren do. Similar results were reported for adults (Rushton & Jensen, 2005: Suzuki & Valencia, 1997). For better comprehension of the differences between some of the groups, just imagine that the average white person tests higher than about 80 percent of the population of blacks and an average black person tests higher than about 20 percent of the population of whites. According to studies, some racial-group differences in IQ appear in early childhood. For example, on the Differential Aptitude Battery, by age 6, the average IQ of East Asian children was 107, compared with 103 for white children and 89 for black children (Lynn, 1996). The size of the average black-white difference does not change significantly over the developmental period from three years of age and beyond.

The mean intelligence test scores for Latino groups are usually between those of blacks and whites. If we divide U.S. citizens along their religions, we will find that Jews, and specifically Jews of European origin, test higher than any other religious group in the United States. Studies of Korean and Vietnamese children adopted into white homes in the United States show that they tend to grow to have IQs 10 or more points higher than their adoptive national norms (Rushton & Jensen, 2005). Even though it is established that Americans of Japanese, Chinese, and Korean ancestry have higher scores than American whites, there is no consistency in research findings. The differences in scores that do occur are usually in the low single digits. The average difference between black and white IQ scores is established at every level of the socioeconomic ladder. In other words, upper-class blacks have lower test scores than upper-class whites, and lower-class whites have higher lost scores than lower-class blacks. Cultural disparities in cognitive performance are found around the world. In India, members of the higher castes obtain higher mean scores and examination marks than do those of the lower castes. In Malaysia, members of the Chinese and East Indian minority communities have higher mean scores than those of the majority Malay population. In South Africa, members of the white, East Indian, and colored population groups obtain higher mean scores than members of the indigenous black African majority (Lynn & Vanhanen, 2002).

Some groups are found to have higher scores on certain scales and lower scores on others. For instance, the verbal intelligence scores of Native Americans were found to be lower than these same scores were for other ethnic groups. However, some studies showed the existence of high visual-spatial skills in Native American groups (McShane & Berry, 1988). East Asians score slightly higher than whites on nonverbal intelligence and equal or slightly lower on verbal intelligence. Moreover, studies suggest that the visual and spatial abilities of East Asians are superior to their verbal abilities, despite substantial political and socioeconomic differences among East Asian countries (Herrnstein & Murray, 1994).

EXPLAINING GROUP DIFFERENCES IN TEST SCORES: INTELLIGENCE AND INTELLIGENT BEHAVIOR

In an attempt to explain some group differences on intelligence test scores, Sternberg (1997) suggested distinguishing between intelligence and intelligent behavior. Intelligence, from his standpoint, is a mental process that may or may not result in particular behavioral responses. These behaviors vary from culture to culture. Something considered intelligent among members of one culture may not be viewed as such in other cultures. If a Washingtonian knows how to negotiate the conditions of a three-year lease with a car dealer, this skill may not be—and likely will not be—very useful at a farm market in Istanbul or Helsinki. Dealing with different cultural contexts, people develop different cognitive skills and acquire dissimilar ways of thinking and learning that are useful in their particular cultural environment. Take, for example, the way people use categories to describe their experience. Traditionally, among navigators in Southeast Asia, the word "south" is often used to refer only to "seaward," which can be any side of the horizon (Frake, 1980). This centuries-old understanding of directions is inappropriate and confusing to visiting foreigners.

However, people may share some general understandings about what intelligence is because the underlying psychological mechanisms of intelligence are expected to be quite similar in all individuals. Among these processes are abilities to understand a problem, identify its type, prepare a solution, find resources to solve the problem, manage the process of solution, and, finally, evaluate the outcome of behavior. Nevertheless—and this is a key element in the understanding intelligent behavior—the specific content of such behavior in each of these stages is determined by the specific environment in which the individual lives (Farhi, 2007). A chess master in India uses these strategies to make particular moves on a chessboard, whereas a farmer in Bosnia, using the same psychological mechanisms, secures a good deal buying a new tractor.

Reasoning that is causal, scientific, and based on empirical facts is not applicable in all cultures all the time (Shea, 1985). A ritualistic dance of a Brazilian tribesman may be considered "unintelligent" behavior by many people in London or Tokyo: "Look at him, he is dancing to stop the rain," some taunt sarcastically. These same taunting individuals, however, go every week to their temples and churches and, by doing this, commit themselves to similar ritualistic acts. Moral? People develop cognitive skills best adapted to the needs of their lifestyle (Dasen et al., 1979).

DO BIOLOGICAL FACTORS CONTRIBUTE TO INTELLIGENCE?

According to the **nativist view**, most cognitive phenomena are inborn. They unravel as a result of biological "programming," and environmental perception requires little active construction by the organism. Hypothetically, according to this view, a boy in Nepal and a girl in Venezuela are both expected to develop some elements of conceptual thinking by approximately the age of seven. No one can make these children think conceptually when they are four years old. This view argues that hereditary factors determine both the depth and scope of our intellectual skills.

These are not just the empty statements of a handful of researchers. In the 1980s, two scientists asked more than 1,000 scholars to give their opinion about IQ, in particular about the differences in IQ scores among ethnic groups. Even though only 1 percent suggested that the differences are always caused by genetic factors, almost 45 percent of the professionals reported that the differences are the product of both genetic and environmental variations (many could not or did not want to give a definitive answer). Remarkably, of all those interviewed only one in seven said that the difference is entirely due to environmental factors (Snyderman & Rothman, 1988). French neuroscientist Stanislas Dehaene (2002) maintains that the mathematical ability of humans may be imbedded in the brain and could be generally independent of memory and reasoning. Moreover, an individual's learning experience, school programs, and even spoken language (like French) may even suppress the development of certain inborn mathematical skills. Dehaene also argues that some languages, like Chinese, may be more helpful to develop a person's basic natural mathematical abilities.

Further support to the assumption that an individual's ability to be successful on cognitive tests is somehow biologically "programmed" and may be less dependent on this person's educational effort comes from a study conducted by Derek Briggs (2001). He found that young people who take preparation courses for college admission tests (such as the SAT in the United States) show only a small improvement in their scores. In other words, whether people study for this test or not, the results of these two groups are likely to be the same. Although some critics reasoned that the conclusions of this study simply pointed out the little effectiveness of the preparation courses, others suggested that certain cognitive skills cannot be improved over a short period of time, which indicates the existence of "deeper" roots of these skills.

There is evidence that heredity plays an important role in human intelligence. For example, the intelligence scores of identical twins raised either together or apart correlate almost +0.90 (Bouchard et al., 1990). One study of 543 pairs of identical twins and 134 pairs of nonidentical twins in Japan reported a substantial heritability of 0.58 for IQ (Lynn & Hattori, 1990). About two dozen studies conducted using magnetic resonance imaging (MRI) to measure the volume of the human brain have found an overall correlation with IQ (Vernon et al., 2000). Twenty-five percent of cases of mental retardation are caused by known biological defects (Grossman, 1983). Moreover, the intelligence scores of adopted children strongly correlate with the scores of their biological parents, whereas there is only a weak correlation between scores of adoptive parents and adopted children (Munsinger, 1978). The correlation between the IQ scores of two biologically unrelated individuals, who were raised together, is also relatively low: +0.20 (Bouchard & McGue, 1981). It is also known that vocabulary size, or the number of words a person remembers and uses in his or her communications, may depend on genetic predispositions. However, even though various data suggest high correlations between parents and children and brothers and sisters in terms of their intellectual skills, these data tell little about what would happen to people's IQ scores if they lived in a different social context than the one in which they actually grew up. Moreover, genetic links for individual differences and similarities do not imply that group differences—on the national level, for example—are also based on genetic factors (Sternberg, 2004). The fact that the heritability of IQ is high does not mean that individual differences in intellectual functioning are permanent. It shows that some individuals are probably genetically predisposed to be more teachable, more trainable, and more capable of learning skills than others, under current conditions and within specific cultural contexts (Lynn & Hattori, 1990).

Besides genetic factors, cross-cultural psychologists examine how particular environmental conditions affect human physiology and whether such biological changes influence cognitive skills. It was found, for instance, that the presence or absence of a particular chemical in a specific geographic region might have affected the overall cognitive performance of the population living in that territory. To illustrate, iodine-deficient areas are found in some regions of Indonesia as well as in Spain. Clinicians report that substantial iodine deficiency in the human body can cause severe mental and neurological abnormalities (see Bleichrodt et al., 1980). In accordance with predictions, cognitive test scores obtained from children living in iodine-deficient areas of Spain and Indonesia were much lower than the scores obtained from children residing in neighboring areas where the water contained sufficient amounts of iodine.

From the previous reading, we learn that psychological mechanisms of intelligence are quite similar in every person regardless of cultural background. On a general level, **intelligence** is our ability or abilities involved in learning and adaptive behavior (Morris and

Figure 5.2

Maisto 2016). The behaviors we use to learn and adapt vary between cultures, however. What shows intelligence in one culture may be seen as unintelligent in another. *Intelligence cannot be defined outside of one's culture.* If a skilled hunter is able to provide for an entire village, he or she may be seen as highly intelligent. If one is able to heal or guide others, he or she may be known as the "wise one."

How is intelligence defined in American culture? I've asked this question many times to groups of college students. Here are some of the quick replies: One who has degrees in education, one who makes a lot of money, one who is able to do difficult math and science problems quickly, or one who speaks many languages. Some cultures believe that if a problem is done quickly, it's detrimental and irresponsible. Many believe taking your time to reflect and ponder on how to approach and resolve a problem is a more intelligent approach. How is intelligence defined in a remote African village where people work together to survive by raising crops, hunting, telling stories, and creating baskets and jewelry? Their definition of what makes one intelligent will certainly differ from the American perspective.

As you can see in Figure 5.2, Howard Gardner has identified eight different types of intelligences, including mathematical-logical, linguistic, spatial, musical, bodily-kinesthetic, interpersonal, intrapersonal, and naturalistic. Later, existential intelligence was added to Gardner's list. Please watch the following video clips from the documentary *Master of the Killer Ants*. What types of intelligences do you notice, and how do they differ from Americans' view of intellect?

 https://www.youtube.com/watch?v=s2XOhcXz_zs

 https://www.youtube.com/watch?v=6dTeB6q0rNc

 https://www.youtube.com/watch?v=4WjBWK21-Cc

 https://www.youtube.com/watch?v=xKDJptuu8eU

There is so much to be learned from this documentary in addition to our topic of intelligence such as parenting, gender roles, education, and societal rules. What can we learn from the Mofu tribe? What stands out about their way of life? Hopefully we can learn from this the benefit of identifying several types of intelligence.

Figure 5.3 Emotional strengths are also recognized as a specific type of intelligence.

Self-Awareness
Emotional Self-Awareness
Accurate Self-Assessment
Self-Confidence

Social Awareness
Empathy
Organizational Awareness
Service Orientation

Emotional Intelligence

Relationship Management
Developing Others
Inspirational Leadership
Conflict Management

Self-Management
Emotional Self-Control
Initiative
Optimism

Copyright © Depositphotos/vaeenma.

WHAT DOES THIS MEAN TO ME?

Consider your strengths and weaknesses. Have you ever thought of yourself as less intelligent based on past experiences in school or perhaps interactions with parents or teachers? Do your interests or strengths fall outside of what others would see as being "intelligent" in our culture? Do you look at others and make judgements about their intellect based on academic performance in certain subjects? Take time to consider that we all have intelligence in certain areas. Based on Gardner's multiple intelligences, what can you personally identify with the most, and in what way are you able to utilize your strengths to the benefit of yourself and others?

There are two types of intelligence that are not included in Gardner's theory that other researchers have brought to light. Daniel Goldman proposed a theory of emotional intelligence, which refers to how emotion is perceived and understood, including one's own emotions and the emotions of others. You can see in Figure 5.3 that there are many facets of emotional intelligence that can deeply impact our interaction with others. Sternberg (mentioned earlier) included creativity and insight as important elements in human intelligence (Morris and Maisto 2016). Creativity such as painting, philosophy, or other socially valued ideas are usually overlooked when discussing intelligence. In addition, it's very unlikely that traditional intelligence assessments would include creative or interpersonal characteristics. There are, however, specific tests that may be done to evaluate emotional and creative intelligence.

EDUCATION

Figure 5.4 Education can take many forms worldwide.

Copyright © Depositphotos/Steve_Allen.

A society's educational system is one of the most important ways that cultural values are taught and reinforced. What is important to a culture will be the same values that are taught in school. Notice that in the *Master of the Killer Ants* documentary, understanding and learning everything about the environment is crucial to the success and happiness of the entire village. In this culture, it was very appropriate for the young children to learn about termites. They were also part of a post figurative culture where the elders of the village teach them through story and daily activities.

Research shows that American students are lagging behind in math and science scores especially when compared to many Asian cultures. Are the students in cultures with higher math and science scores smarter than students here in America? Of course not; but we do differ greatly in what is emphasized in our education. "Different cultures believe different topics to be important for later success in that society. By teaching a certain type of content, the educational system reinforces a particular view of cognition and intelligence" (Matsumoto and Juang 2013). Asian parents, for example, may focus more on effort in learning and receiving good grades while American parents tend to focus on a child's ability and encourage him or her in the direction of his or her natural strengths.

The environmental setting involved in a child's education also varies between cultures. In more formal settings, students are seated in a classroom with a certified teacher to pass on what is usually a preset curriculum. In some societies, the elders may talk to youth in small groups in an outdoor setting. One of the best ways to learn is to actually do activities that teach important concepts. For example, in some island cultures, such as Micronesia, children are taught math skills through navigation. Ghanaians living on the coast will learn through marketing fish. (Acioly and Schliemann 1986; Gladwin 1970; Gladwin and Gladwin 1971). Many children work with their parents to learn valuable skills that are important to their own culture. Mastsumoto and Juang (2013) make a conclusion about cultural education in the following excerpt.

> Regardless of the way education occurs, the choices a society and culture make concerning its structure, organization, planning, and implementation all encourage and reinforce a certain view of culture. We are not always cognizant of our own cultural view because we are in the middle of it. To see our own biases and choices, we need to observe education in other cultures and compare what is done elsewhere to what we do. Through such comparisons, the differences and similarities often become quite clear.

It is clear, that as humans, we all have the ability to think and learn. Our enculturation and environment will determine *how* we think and *what* we learn. As humans, we are driven to thrive and are taught those behaviors that will allow us to adapt to our own cultures. Once we accept that we all have our own way of adapting that includes different perceptions and abilities, we will understand that there is no single definition of intelligence. Just as we all possess individual strengths and weaknesses, so do groups of people around the world, sharing collective strengths and abilities based on their experiences and cultural settings.

Chapter 6

Culture and Emotion

Human behavior flows from three main sources: desire, emotion, and knowledge.

—Plato

Figure 6.1

A newborn child, the death of a loved one, or obtaining a goal may all elicit intense feelings within any individual. In fact, it would be hard to imagine living our lives without these feelings. To be without emotion, some would agree, would be a life not worth living. The concept of human emotion has been monopolizing the minds of many ancient philosophers. Emotion has also been the theme for much of our art, music, poetry, and many historical events. The *scientific* study of human emotion however, has a much shorter time span that began just over a hundred years ago.

Emotion is a response that typically includes a physiological arousal, a subjective experience (either positive, negative, or ambivalent), then followed by a behavioral expression

85

(Shiraev and Levy 2013). Emotion is a fascinating topic especially when comparing and contrasting cultures. Are emotions universal? Certainly we have recognized facial expressions regardless of cultural background. Do we learn emotion from our own culture or are these feelings and expressions innate? David Matsumoto, an expert in this field, explains this topic in the following video clip.

https://www.youtube.com/watch?v=5G6ZR5lJgTI

BIOLOGY OF HUMAN EMOTION

As we have learned, there are similar emotions and expressions found worldwide. Even people who have never seen these expressions (like the blind athletes in the video clip) were able to make the same facial expressions with the emotions they were experiencing. This is strong evidence that facial expressions are genetically encoded and not learned through social interaction. The physiology of emotions and their expressions are explained further in the following excerpt by Krum Krumov and Knud S. Larsen (2013) in their book *Why Culture Matters*.

Reading 6.1

THE UNIVERSALITY OF EMOTIONS: BASIC NEUROPHYSIOLOGICAL RESPONSES

Emotions are closely connected to specific physiological reactions in the auto-nomic and central nervous systems. Ekman, Levenson, and Friesen (1983) found that basic emotions produce distinct and discrete signals in the autonomic sys-tem. Others have also found specific emotion related responses in the central nervous system (Davidson, Pizzagalli, Nitschke, & Kalin, 2003; Mauss, Levenson, McCarter, Wilhelm, & Gross, 2005). *Research has also demonstrated similar neu-rophysiological responses for the basic emotions in cross-cultural samples dem-onstrating their universality (Tsai & Levenson, 1997).*

Researchers in biology and neurosciences have in the past also tried to locate the locus of emotions in certain brain structures (Gazzaniga, 1995). As might be expected it is not an easy process to find the emotion pathway in specific brain locations for complex subjective feelings of anger, sadness or happiness and the biological locus of these emotions are not well understood (Cacioppo & Tassinary, 1990). Neverthe-less research has demonstrated convincingly the relationship between emotions and biological processes. Darwin (1998) argued that human behavior evolved from earlier primate ancestors and emotions exist as part of our behavioral repertoire since they serve evolutionary adaptation. In particular emotions serve the function of supporting adaptive fitness by providing important information about our subjective states, our relationships to others, and the emotion stimuli.

Over the years researchers have concluded that basic emotions (anger, fear, dis-gust, sadness, happiness, and surprise) are hardwired in the human brain. Basic emo-tions are thought to have evolved as part of our genetic inheritance and have cer-tain characteristics in common (Ekman, 1992; Matsumoto & Hwang, 2011). The basic emotions are identified by universally recognized signals that are also present in other primates. As noted these responses produce collateral changes in the autonomic and central nervous systems, are related to distinctive antecedent events, and dem-onstrate coherence in reactions. Basic emotions are rapid in onset, of brief duration, and are typically appraised automatically.

HOW WE UNDERSTAND THE EMOTION OF OTHERS: FACIAL EXPRESSIONS

In his original research Darwin argued that humans all over the world use exactly the same facial expressions to convey emotions. According to Darwinian Theory facial expressions are a part of our biological inheritance and are adaptive by conveying important emotional information. Darwin also noted that we share with the great apes some of similar facial expressions a finding that support our common evolutionary path with other primates. Ethologists (Snowdon, 2003) have produced evidence for the universality and genetic basis of facial expressions in the primates. For example, there are many morphological similarities between primate and human expressions when evaluated in similar social contexts. Some research found that infant chimpanzee has similar facial expressions as human infants (Ueno, Ueno, & Tomonaga, 2004). *Facial expressions provide a communication context to emotions thereby serving adaptive functions in intergroup and interpersonal behavior.* Ekman, (1973) however, noted that the common experiences of human infants might also provide a basis for universal human expressions and that therefore universality can only be inferred from controlled experiments. Universality, however, is supported by the research on human development. The facial musculature necessary for facial expressions is present and functional at birth (Ekman & Oster, 1979). Infants are capable of signaling their emotional states and show interest and attention (Oster, 2005). The presence of universal emotional expressions so early in development is evidence of their biological basis.

Early studies (Ekman, 1972; Izard, 1971) independently pioneered a methodology to investigate the universality of the ability to recognize facial expressions of human emotions. Ekman created a series of photographs of facial expressions thought to represent universal basic emotions recognizable in every culture. Respondents in five countries were presented and asked to provide a label for photographs that corresponded to the six common emotions of happiness, anger fear, disgust, sadness and surprise. Later (Ekman & Friesen, 1986) added contempt to the universally recognized expressions list. The results showed a very broad agreement identifying the same emotional expressions from the photographs among the judges from all cultures. Furthermore there were no significant differences in facial recognition between respondents from the different cultures. However, the respondents in these early studies all came from advanced industrialized societies leading critics to suggest that concordance in agreement might be the result of cultural diffusion in the display of emotion caused by Western movies and other media. The critics concluded that cultural diffusion and not biology contributed to the apparent universality of emotion display.

Ekman and his colleagues conducted another study (Ekman, Sorenson, & Friesen, 1969) employing similar methodology with preliterate tribes of New Guinea in an attempt to find respondents isolated from Western culture. Rather than asking for language labels that might not be available to the respondents Ekman requested that the participants tell a story illustrating the facial expression in the photographs. The results were remarkably similar to the labeling experiments as the stories were concordant with the emotions illustrated in the photographs. Cultural experience moderated responses to a small degree since recognition of emotions for children were very high around 90 percent, but lower for adults (80 percent). However, since these preliterate societies could not have experienced cultural diffusion, or at least only in very limited ways, the results were accepted as confirming the universality of emotions.

Later Ekman and his colleagues asked the tribe members to demonstrate emotions with their own facial expressions and took photographs of these responses. The facial expressions of the tribe members were then shown to American respondents who again correctly labeled the emotions displayed in the new tribal photographs supporting universality. Izard (1971) independently examined the issue of the universality of facial recognition. In general his results supported those found by Ekman and his colleagues. Further, Ekman, Friesen, O'Sullivan, Chan, Diacoyanni-Tarlatzis, Heider, Krause, LeCompte, Pitcairn, Ricci-Bitti, Scherer, Tomita, and Tzavaras (1987) in a study of ten cultures found similar universal recognition of even complex blended emotions.

The aforementioned research was based on the assumption that universality can be demonstrated by common cross-cultural agreement in the labeling of or story telling about photographic stimuli. However, will people spontaneously display these basic emotions and are these reactions also universal? A study comparing responses in Japan and the U.S. (Ekman, 1972) exposed respondents to very stressful stimuli while taping their facial reactions. The results showed that the respondents from both countries showed similar facial reactions to the stressful stimuli. The universality of expression and recognition of emotions have now been documented in many research programs and is commonly accepted (Elfenbein & Ambady, 2002; Matsumoto, Keltner, Shiota, Frank, & O'Sullivan, 2008). The basic emotions are expressed very rapidly and apparently with automatic appraisal and little cognitive awareness and are thought to be the product of evolution. The social context can modify responses, but without contextual differences facial expressions are universally similar.

Further, the emotions expressed are recognized in all cultures. Matsumoto (2001) reviewed 27 research reports of facial expressions and found universal recognition of the basic emotions. The meta-analysis reported by Elfenbein and Ambady (2002) also supported the universal recognition of emotion signals produced by facial expressions. It seems indisputable that such common agreement would not be found independent of culture unless the facial expressions were in fact universal and genetically based. Further research has expanded the list of emotions that are universally recognized (Matsumoto & Ekman, 2004; Tracy & Robins, 2004). These studies together support the assertion that humans innately possess basic emotions as part of a genetically determined inheritance.

Figure 6.2 "Emoticons" have added a whole new dimension to our communication, especially among the younger generation.

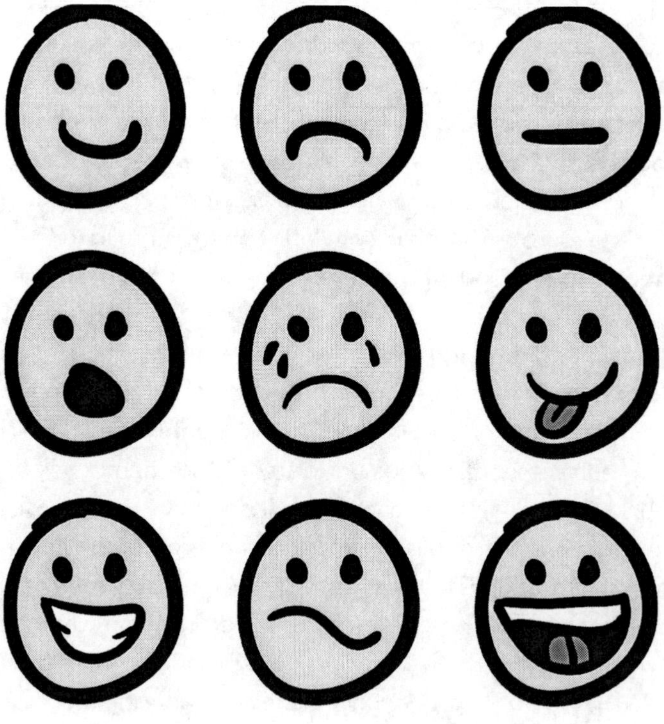

CULTURAL SIMILARITIES IN EMOTIONAL EXPRESSION

What ARE the basic human emotions that have been found globally? *Joy, sadness, surprise, contempt, disgust, anger, and fear* are all universal feelings and expressions (Mastumoto and Juang 2013). It's important to mention, however, that not ALL cultures agree that these are the basic emotions. In the Buddhist tradition, for example, there are also seven emotions, but love, hate, and desire are included in place of a few others. The basic emotions, according to Matsumoto and Juang, have also proven through research to be universally recognized. In other words, we have the genetic ability in the right side of our brain to recognize these facial expressions and emotions.

Basic emotions have an adaptive function. In order for humans to survive and adapt to the environment, these emotions and reactions are "hard-wired" into our brains. Disgust, for example, may prevent us from trying potentially dangerous substances such as rotting food or bad water. Fear elicits a "fight or flight" response system in our bodies that can also protect us from danger (Shiraev and Levy 2013). We have the ability to "read" each other socially, which proves to be a very important survival instinct. Those who do not have the ability to recognize emotional expression will more than likely be at a disadvantage with safety among other relationship challenges.

Emotions and the way they are shown through facial expressions are so important in our relationships and communication with others, that even today with the ever growing lack of face-to-face interaction, we have figured out how to include these expressions in our digitized world. With the implementation of "emoticons," we have improved our communication and are better able to express our thoughts. In fact, one simple display of a digitized facial expression can change the entire meaning of an e-mail or text. Our youth today (in many places around the world) will admit that this is a very important part of their "digital" communication.

UNIVERSAL SIMILARITIES IN EVENTS PRECEDING EMOTION

We know that every individual experiences the same basic emotions, but are they aroused in the same way? The most prominent research done with emotional antecedents across cultures was that of Scherer and colleagues (Scherer and Wallbott 1994), who conducted a number of studies using questionnaires designed to assess the quality and nature of emotional experiences in many different cultures. The following is a summary of their research findings.

Happiness or Joy	Attaining a goal or accomplishment
Sadness	Losing a loved one or something of value

Anger	Being prevented from attaining a goal/mistreatment
Surprise	New or novel objects
Fear	A threat to psychological or physical safety
Disgust	Contamination
Contempt	Moral superiority

You may recognize that there are so many other scenarios that could cause these emotions that are not listed. While the details surrounding these activities will vary, the underlying and basic causes are the same. Which goal is attained may vary among cultures. For instance, happiness in some cultures may be a successful hunting trip that would provide food for many, a successful crop that will feed others for a season, or having a large family. Happiness in America may mean earning a degree or landing a well-paying job. What food item one finds disgusting in one culture may be a delicacy in another, but whatever causes one to fear contamination, in some way, will experience disgust.

CULTURAL DIFFERENCES IN EMOTIONAL EXPRESSION

There are seven basic emotions and facial expressions in which we experience a human, physiological reaction. But what are some of the differences in emotions and emotional displays cross-culturally? Every culture has its own unwritten rules and expectations regarding how someone *should* feel in a certain situation and how emotions *should* be displayed. **Cultural display rules** are a guideline for how emotions should be displayed within a culture and are learned from the socialization process from birth. Imagine going to a Middle-Eastern or Asian country and showing physical affection for your spouse or significant other on a public street. This action could be extremely disrespectful and maybe even punishable in some areas. Many of my international students, when asked what behaviors are difficult to adjust to here in America, often mention the displays of affection they observe in public. They say they feel uncomfortable and that it feels inappropriate. In contrast, many American students hardly notice it and in most cases, don't feel offended or embarrassed when witnessing it.

It can be assumed that one attending a funeral or ceremony for a deceased loved one will feel sadness. Although feelings of sadness may be similar in this setting, we can still witness great cultural differences in the way this emotion is displayed. In some locations around the world, it's appropriate and respectful to abstain from showing outward emotion, and in others, NOT showing enough emotion could equal disrespect, and your love for the deceased could be in question. The first time I experienced a cultural difference in emotional display at a funeral, I was a bit shocked and remember feeling uneasy. Upon doing a little research on the cultural background of those who were mourning and crying, I quickly learned that their behavior was appropriate and respectful to the deceased and the survivors based on their cultural norms. Gaining just a little bit of information on the situation changed my whole perspective on what I had witnessed. Learning about these differences leads to more understanding and tolerance.

In some areas, it may be considered a weakness to show emotion. Not controlling your emotions, however justified they may be, can bring shame to yourself and to your family. Furthermore, collectivistic cultures may be more concerned with how an individual emotional display may affect others involved. Thinking in terms of "what's most beneficial for the group" can strongly influence the emotional behavior of an individual. The following paragraph explains some differences between ethnic groups found through research.

Figure 6.3 In some cultures, public displays of affection may be offensive and violate cultural display rules.

Copyright © Depositphotos/lucidwaters.

Studying stress in African Americans, Jenkins (1995) suggested that blacks may have developed a special emotional style of behavioral response that reflects the cultural value placed on the individual's ability to manage stressful life events. In African American culture, from the author's view, emphasis is placed on the active managing of difficult situations without displaying nervous tension. Thus, a difference between European Americans and African Americans may be found in their emotional assessments of reality. In blacks, their emotionality is displayed more often than it is in whites. This type of African American emotional response may be passed on from generation to generation as a cultural norm (Shiraev and Levy 2013).

The author goes on to explain that self-critical, pessimistic evaluation of one's own life may be viewed as a cultural norm in other ethnic groups. Older Russian immigrants, for example, have a higher level—in comparison to other groups—of negative emotions including anxiety and sadness (Consedine and Magai 2002). Another difference can be seen in social settings. From a Western perspective, the absence of anxiety in social situations is seen as desirable and associated with positive mental health and healthy interpersonal functioning. With a contrasting Asian perspective, a certain level of anxiety about social situations may be normal and even desirable (Okazaki et al. 2002).

There are myriad reasons as to *why* these differences exist between groups which could be discussed in more detail; however, I want to keep in line with my goal of offering introductory information in this text. I will conclude this section by stating that it's important to keep in mind that because of our cultural environment and our everyday lives, our attitudes and emotions, and the way in which they are displayed may vary from culture to culture.

WHAT DOES THIS MEAN TO ME?

Consider your own cultural background and how you have been taught to show emotion. Were you taught to be open and to display the way you feel? If so, how did you react when first confronted with someone who did NOT want to show emotion? How did you assess the situation: were you offended, questioned your relationship, or wondered why he or she was being so rude? Are you one to abstain from showing your emotion? If so, does it make you feel uncomfortable when you are around someone who does show his or her emotion or who may be more physically affectionate? Is it common for you to smile as a way to say hello when passing by someone? Have you ever been exposed to others who do NOT readily smile and wondered why they're unhappy? A lack of a smile, eye contact, or personal touch may be a sign of respect based on that individual's or group's cultural norms. Take time to account for cultural differences in your personal and work relationships, and watch your appreciation for others who differ grow.

Figure 6.4 Abraham Maslow proposed the theory of a "hierarchy of needs." We can obtain a higher level of development only after our fundamental needs have been met.

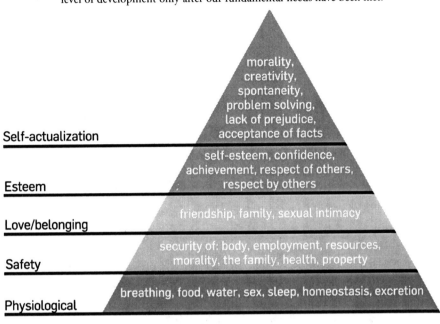

THE LOCATION OF EMOTION

Read the following excerpt from *Culture and Psychology* regarding the differences in our perception of emotion.

> To Americans, emotions are located inside oneself. To Samoans, Pintupi aborigines and Solomon Islanders, emotions are statements about relationships among people or between people and events. The African Fulani concept "semteende," which is commonly translated as shame or embarrassment, refers more to a situation than to a feeling; that is, if the situation is appropriate to "semteende," then someone is feeling it, regardless of what any one individual actually feels (Riesman 1977).

This idea may be hard for us to understand because emotion in the Western part of the world is thought more to be something *felt* by a person and not a reference to a situation. Also, the place in the body where emotion is felt has some cultural differences as well. Most Americans will say that emotion may be felt in the chest or the heart. Other cultures may think of emotion as felt more in the abdomen or the gut. Tahitians locate emotions as arising from the intestines (Levy 1973). Some cultures don't even have a word for "emotion" as we do. Ifaluk is the language spoken in Micronesia. The closest Ifaluk word to the English word *emotion* is *niferash*, which translates as "our insides" (Lutz 1982).

HAPPINESS

It's our human nature to strive for happiness and belonging. Cultural differences will lie in *what* events or situations will create happiness and exactly what activities *precede* becoming a competent and productive member of society. Abraham Maslow (1970), a humanistic psychologist, arranged a pattern of individual needs that must be met in order to progress to a personally fulfilling level of human growth and happiness.

We will not be concerned with our social group or status if we are trying to find food and water to survive (see image 6.4). While there are some who criticize Maslow's "hierarchy of needs" on a basic level, it does make sense that striving for happiness through self-esteem and personal achievement cannot happen if our basic needs are not met. We have a human will to survive, and all of our time and energy will be spent on that aspect first. Once our physiological and safety needs are met, we may then focus on our family and community. When we have a strong family and community base, we can continue to progress. We may begin to understand where we fit in our group and what contributions that we may make as an individual. We may go as far as accomplishing our personal goals and refining who we are by learning more about ourselves and others in the world.

How does knowing this benefit us? Understanding that there are different levels of progression based on these needs can help us as we come in contact with, or work with others from around the world or even in our own community. We need to be mindful of those faced with the task of providing the basic needs for survival. Being in a survival mode will definitely affect thoughts, behaviors, and relationships.

What is happiness and how is it defined? If we can begin to look outside of our own schema and open our eyes to the worldviews of others, we may see that happiness can be achieved in so many different ways.

Here's one interesting way that a country strives for happiness. Take a look at the following video clips to determine what is most important in some cultures.

http://www.youtube.com/watch?v=7Zqdqa4YNvI

 http://www.youtube.com/watch?v=CXJwNSkdTH0

Here is another perspective of what happiness is according to Nic Marcs.

 https://www.youtube.com/watch?v=M1o3FS0awtk

Who are the happiest nations and why? There are so many things to consider when talking about happiness in a particular place. There are environmental influences on one's happiness such as physical environment, economics, government, and resources, but much of the research will base the idea of happiness on equality, sustainability, and freedom of choice. Those who express the most satisfaction with life usually have freedom to choose how they will live their life. Those who live in the unhappiest countries usually struggle for survival but also lack the freedom (usually through corrupt governments, inequality, or strong precedence of a caste system) to choose how they live and lack hope for any personal progress or development.

What's amazing is how many people on the earth have so little in the way of material possessions yet find joy by focusing on the "silver linings" of life. Just as so many behaviors are learned and passed down to future generations, so are attitudes and views of the meaning of life and our place in the world. Some will say that happiness is a state of mind and a personal choice while others will claim that outside circumstances are the biggest influence on whether one will experience a joyful or a miserable life. What mindset will you pass on to those in your life who follow you?

Learning each other's attitudes (whether it's positive or negative) and why we feel the way we do, can give us a deeper insight and understanding of how cultures differ and an opportunity to assess our own values and attitudes on life. This may bring us one step closer to the top of Maslow's pyramid by understanding ourselves through learning more about others—the way we react to life's events, the way we respond to our environment, and the way we express ourselves emotionally.

Culture and Communication

To effectively communicate, we must realize that we are all different in the way we perceive the world and use this understanding as a guide to our communication with others.

—Anthony Robbins

Figure 7.1

Copyright © Depositphotos/depositedhar.

LANGUAGE

Although animals have the ability to communicate, verbal language is unique to humans. All human infants are able to make the same basic sounds called *morphemes*. Through socialization in a culture, certain sounds are emphasized and become strengthened. Of all aspects of cross-cultural study, language and culture, in my opinion, have the strongest link to each other. **Our culture influences our language from an early age, and our language strongly influences our culture**. A shared language has the ability to draw people together but is also one of the biggest barriers *between* groups of people all over the world. Our unique use of words and sounds constructs the way we view the world. As shared in the chapter on culture and cognition, we can literally view the world differently based on our language as we saw with the Himba tribe and its perception of color based on its use of words for different hues in the environment.

Most of us have tried at some point, to communicate with someone who speaks a different language. As we know, this can prove to be very challenging. For most immigrants and refugees, the task of learning a new language can be overwhelming. Translating a language is helpful, but even when words are translated, using one word over another or pronouncing words differently can change the entire meaning. Consider for a moment words in the English language. If someone says the word "iron," is he or she referring to an iron to press clothes or the element iron that is found in the earth? This may or may not be solved by the context in which it used. In Spanish the word "caliente" means hot, but the word "calor" means heat. Although very similar, the use of these words is different and using one over the other can cause confusion. Another problem arises when there just aren't the right words to convey the meaning intended. Many times the translators, though well meaning, will change the phrase for better understanding but affect the integrity of the desired message or question which can ultimately affect the goals of the research.

BILINGUALISM

Speaking more than one language has many benefits. By learning another language, we can acquire more understanding of our own language and have the ability to learn through the increased capacity to interact with others who speak that language. Having the skill to speak two or more languages may also open doors for employment. Those who speak more than one language however, may find it difficult not to refer to specific words from another language when trying to communicate effectively. There may be a lull in the conversation as the speaker is searching for the right word to use and then finds that there isn't a direct translation for it! Many times the speaker will just use the word from the other language and then take a second to describe what it means. In addition to having a few mix-ups or frustrations, those who speak two or more languages have some other challenges they must face as well. People who speak in a different language may draw negative impressions and stereotypes based on their response time and seem to have more cognitive difficulties while processing information. These difficulties are referred to as **foreign language processing difficulties** (Matsumoto and Juang 2013). I have been told from some parents over the years that although they immigrated from another country and speak another language, they prefer to teach their children just one language. Some parents who face foreign language processing difficulties themselves, want their children to become strong with just one language and fear that by learning two they may be weaker in both languages being learned.

Because language and culture are so strongly intertwined, those who speak a particular language may actually think and behave differently based on the language they are speaking! Differences in personality were found through studies done with immigrant bilinguals (Hull 1987; Dinges and Hull 1992). These students were given a personality test called the California Psychological Inventory (CPI). They took the test twice—once in their native language and once in the foreign language. Researchers were interested to discover that they indeed showed signs of two different personalities depending on whether it was their native language or foreign language used. "Immigrants are believed to have two clearly distinct cultural affiliations, accessible through the language in which much of this cultural knowledge was learned or is associated" (Matsumoto and Juang 2013).

OTHER CHALLENGES IN VERBAL COMMUNICATION

Although cultures may speak the same language, there are still obstacles in communication. I learned the hard way that the words "fanny pack" and "bugger" are offensive to some from England and neighboring areas. I was surprised to learn that the word "idiot," while relatively insulting in the U.S., is not as harsh in the U.K. Imagine my surprise when a small child called his father an "idiot," and the father laughed and tickled him afterward! I would not have dreamed of calling my father an "idiot." Not only would it have been disrespectful, but I would have feared the consequences. There are other words (and phrases) that we have in America that are misunderstood in Britain and vice versa. Words such as "knickers," "pissed," and "bombed" all have differing meanings in the U.K. than they do in America and could easily be the root of confusion and frustration. English-speaking Australians as well, have words and phrases that have differing meanings in the U.S. While it may be easier to communicate using the same language in another culture, it certainly does not guarantee a smooth and effortless verbal interaction.

The way things are pronounced can create an issue as well. There are often different dialects in a language, and stereotypes and biases can spring from these differences. An accent from the southern part of the United States may conjure up negative ideas about one's intelligence. An English accent on the other hand, for many Americans may equate to intelligence and class. In some cultures, even within the same language, a different dialect can have a divisive effect among groups of people. As always, it's important to do some research before traveling even if you will be speaking the same language. American students have a reputation for being ignorant of languages other than English (Matsumoto and Juang

2013). This in turn, leads to an ethnocentric view of other cultures and a lack of interest in learning to appreciate and understand other languages and customs. The study of other cultures through traveling, learning a new language, or attending cultural events can open minds and encourage equality and understanding.

MULTI-CULTURAL COMMUNICATION

As time goes on and our digital world brings us closer together, many of us are experiencing more opportunities to associate with people from other cultures. This is especially true in business settings and in the medical field. With so many different cultural backgrounds, it can be a challenge to be sensitive to differences. For example, some cultures use humor while others may not understand it. Listen to the following clip of Dr. Jon Oommen, who explains in more detail the relevance of speaking to groups of people. While his views are taken from a Christian perspective, he feels the importance of being sensitive to ALL groups of people. What is most impressive is Dr. Oommen's ability to remain who he is (which in this case is a

Figure 7.2 To be effective when speaking to a group, it's necessary to be aware of cultural backgrounds.

Christian healthcare provider) but also to show a heightened sensitivity to those around him when he conveys important information. Listen for the three main objectives he offers when speaking to a multi-cultural group.

https://vimeo.com/20226021

Opportunities will arise for many of us to address groups of people whether we are traveling, training, teaching, brainstorming, or working on projects together. Being culturally sensitive and adjusting our behaviors to benefit the group, is crucial to the success and personal well-being of everyone involved. We tend to avoid situations with people of different cultural backgrounds for various reasons (which will be discussed in more detail in a later chapter). We should try to be aware of our words, thoughts, and behaviors when dealing with differing cultural backgrounds. The quote at the beginning of this chapter corresponds to our ability to communicate effectively with insight and understanding.

Figure 7.3 Even the most subtle body movements and facial expressions can convey meaning.

Copyright © Depositphotos/iphemant.

NONVERBAL ASPECTS OF LANGUAGE

What we do physically while we are speaking is crucial to the communication process but can have significant cultural variations. The following information from *Multicultural Psychology* explains some cultural differences and principles in communication.

Reading 7.1

PROXEMICS

proxemics—personal space in conversations.

Proxemics deals with personal space. When people interact with one another, they keep a standard range of distance between them. The range of distance varies depending on the context, such as a close, intimate relationship or a public lecture (Hall, 1966, 1976). In normal conversations the distance between two conversational partners is usually about 1½ feet. According to Hall, the acceptable distance is 1½ to 4 feet. However, numerous studies have found that conversational partners in other cultures tend to stand or sit closer to each other when interacting than do those in the United States and other Western countries (Dolphin, 1999; Matsumoto, 2000). Goldman (1980) found that individuals in the United States feel more uncomfortable when someone stands too close than when he or she stands too far away. I (JSM) recall being at a sporting event and feeling uncomfortable when I saw two sports reporters standing extremely close to one another. I remember thinking how interesting it was that I was the one who was feeling uncomfortable in just *observing* these two people standing so close to one another when they were talking to each other. I then realized that in the context of televised sporting events, they had to stand close to one another in order to both be in the camera shot on television. After I realized the context, I felt much more comfortable about their distance from one another. A student of ours talked about her discomfort about her personal space being violated when she visited her parents' home country of Korea:

> When we talked about how we have cultural norms that govern personal space, I remembered my visit to Korea last winter. I despised

Koreans for having no personal spaces. When I was taking [the] bus or subway, people not only violated my personal space, they were touching me. I hated how my arms had to touch other people's arms. Most of the public transportations were so crowded that I sometimes felt the person behind me breathing. Also, there was one time a Korean grandmother [who] asked me to give my seat to her. She could have just asked and I would have given it to her. She literally put her face in front of my face and told me to move. She spat at me a little and I got really mad. I even told her that nobody talks to me this close, but she did not seem to care at all. I really liked Korea except for there was no personal space and no saying sorry or excuse me. I still do not get that. Even though Korea is a culture that has high respect for elders and has straight rules, I do not know why they do not say sorry or excuse me. I also realized even my close family members in Korea were sitting too close to me when we chat. Although they were my aunts and cousins, I really felt uncomfortable and tried to move as far as I could. I think my family in America adopted the American personal space. When my mom and I talk, we try not to violate each other's personal spaces. I think we know each other's boundaries. It is interesting how my parents unconsciously adopted the American culture.

—Stella, 20+-Year-Old Korean American Woman

Asians tend to stand farther away from each other while talking than their American counterparts. When talking with someone from a different culture, a person can find it difficult to determine a comfortable talking distance. *Photographs by Bikeriderlondon/Shutterstock (left) and Tyler Olsen/ Shutterstock (right)*

Remland, Jones, and Brinkman (1991) studied three European countries (the Netherlands, France, and England). Although some differences were found for pair interaction, such as distance (more distance between Dutch participants, less distance between French pairs, even less distance between English pairs in declining distance) and body orientation (French participants more directly across from each other than Dutch or English participants), no differences were detected when gender and age were examined. In other words, culture was the dominant influence in proxemics in these countries. Some early studies questioned the importance of culture in influencing proxemics (Fortson & Larson, 1968; Mazur, 1977; Shuter, 1977), but more recent studies have confirmed this importance (Mindess, 1999; Sussman & Rosenfeld, 1982; Wolfgang, 1985).

Sue and Sue (2003, 2008, 2013) have given a very practical reason that proxemics is an important topic in multicultural studies. When an individual from a culture that prefers smaller distances between speakers comes in contact with an individual from a culture that prefers larger distances, the first individual might misinterpret the second one's warmth, sincerity, or motive. Imagine a person from a close culture trying to stand closer to a person from a distant culture, who keeps moving away. The person from the close culture may feel that the other is not a very warm person or is trying to hide something, whereas the person from the distant culture may feel that the other is trying to become overly personal or invasive. I (JSM) once greeted an African American friend whom I had not seen in a while. When I reached out to shake his hand, he pulled me closer and gave me a hug, saying, "Come over here like you really know me!" The friendship was close enough that he felt comfortable telling me why he was hugging me, and I felt comfortable enough to give him a hug back. Imagine how it would have seemed if he had tried to give me a hug and I had pulled away.

KINESICS

> kinesics—bodily movements in conversations, including hand gestures, facial expressions, and eye contact.

Sue and Sue (2003, 2008, 2013) define **kinesics** as aspects of communication that deal with bodily movements. This is a wide-ranging category that includes "facial expressions, body movements, gestures, and conversational regulators" (Andersen, 1999, p. 245). One kinesics aspect that has been studied extensively is eye contact or gaze duration. Matsumoto (2000) reported that eye contact can be an indication of either aggression or nurturance, depending on the context. He cites the animal literature as a suggestion of a genetic, animalistic basis for the relation between gaze duration and dominance (see also Matsumoto & Juang, 2012). Certainly, most of us can remember being told as children that it was impolite to stare at someone else. However, equally embedded in our minds are phrases such as "gazing lovingly into someone's eyes" or "casting a loving glance," which indicate that eye contact or gazes can also indicate affection or care. Moreover, there is even evidence that love can be distinguished from lust by evaluating eye gazes (Bolmont, Cacioppo & Cacioppo, in press).

As one might expect, different cultures seem to engage in varying levels of eye contact. Some early studies have found that people from Arabic cultures tend to gaze longer and more directly than do people from the United States (Hall, 1963; Watson & Graves, 1966). Within the United States, African Americans gaze less directly than their European American (White) counterparts (LaFrance & Mayo, 1976). American Indians tend to have even less eye contact (Richardson, 1981) and prefer a side-by-side orientation to a face-to-face orientation. A friend and colleague of ours, Joseph Trimble, once told us,

> When I am interacting with my White colleagues, I sit or stand across from them and interact with them in a manner that is comfortable for them. However, when I visit my friends on the Lakota reservation, I find myself standing side-by-side with them, looking at my feet and kicking at the ground. We rarely look at each other, but we have very good and deep conversations.

> —Joseph Trimble (*Personal Communication*, January 1999)

Now, whenever I (JSM) see Joseph at conferences, I make sure I stand side-by-side. However, not having a great deal of eye contact is different from avoiding eye contact. According to van Meurs and Spencer-Oatey (2010), there are cultural differences in avoidance of eye contact when there is a conflict. Many researchers (e.g., Bond & Hwang, 1986; Ohbuchi & Takahashi, 1994) have labeled this a "neglect style" of dealing with conflict. East Asians tend to have less eye contact under conditions of conflict than their counterparts in the United States. We say "tend to have" because there are large variations in both populations, and among those in the West, van Meurs and Spencer-Oatey reported that

British managers had a more avoidant style of managing than their Dutch counterparts.

Sue and Sue (2003, 2008, 2013) discuss smiling as an important part of kinesics. In general, smiling is an indication of happiness, liking, and other positive feelings. However, Asian cultures may also use smiling as a way of discharging uncomfortable feelings. Ekman (1972) conducted a series of experiments in which he showed American and Japanese students highly stressful videotapes (e.g., of a surgical operation) and secretly videotaped their facial expressions. Half of the time the research participants watched the stressful videotapes alone, and half of the time they watched the videotape with an older, high-status experimenter. The American participants showed facial expressions of disgust, fear, and other negative affects when they watched the film alone or with the experimenter. However, the Japanese participants displayed these negative expressions when watching the videotape alone, but they smiled in the presence of the high-status experimenter. That was because they did not want to offend the experimenter by seeming to disapprove of the task the experimenter was asking them to perform. Thus, although facial expressions of emotion may have some universal application, as evidenced by the similar expressions of the American and Japanese participants when viewing the videotapes alone, the social setting may be an important determinant of the kinesics displayed in a particular situation. Sue and Sue (2013) connected this tendency for Asians to smile when discharging negative emotions with a misunderstanding that arose in the aftermath of the Rodney King verdict during a confrontation between African Americans and Korean grocery store owners:

> African Americans confronted their Korean-American counterparts about exploitation of Black neighborhoods. African Americans became incensed when many Korean American store owners had a constant smile on their faces. They interpreted the facial expression as arrogance, taunting, and lack of compassion for the concerns of Blacks. Little did they realize that a smile in this situation more rightly indicated extreme embarrassment and apprehension. (p. 215)

Kinesics may be determined by the general influences of individualism and collectivism. They tend to be more synchronized in collectivistic cultures (Andersen, 1999; Argyle, 1975), whereas in individualistic cultures, people are allowed to "do their own thing" and not coordinate their movements with others as much. Matsumoto (1991) speculates that "collective cultures will foster emotional displays of their members that maintain and facilitate group cohesion, harmony, or cooperation, to a greater degree than individualistic cultures" (p. 132).

PARALANGUAGE

> paralanguage—nonverbal vocal cues in conversation, such as loud-ness of voice, silences, and rates of speech.

Sue and Sue (2003, 2008, 2013) refer to **paralanguage** as a category that involves the use of nonverbal vocal cues in communication, such as loudness of voice, silences, and rate of speech. Perhaps the aspect of paralanguage that lends itself to the most cultural varia-tion of meaning is silence. In the United States, silences are often signals for the receiver of a message to contribute to the conversation. When silences last too long, people in the United States often become uncomfortable and want to fill in the silence. Many of you have probably heard the expression "pregnant pause," which indicates the discomfort one feels when the conversation has come to a halt and there is an extended period dur-ing which neither conversational partner contributes to the conversation.

However, Hall (1966, 1976) has found that silences mean quite different things in dif-ferent cultures. For example, some cultures (Russian, Spanish) view silences as agreement among the conversational partners. Asian cultures view silence as a sign of respect for elders. For American Indians, silences are a way of gathering one's thoughts, so to break the silence merely disrupts their train of thought. As Richardson (1981) advised when seeing American Indians in a therapy situation,

> Do not lean toward the client and commence giving the "third degree" or studying him or her with piercing eyes. Do not be upset with long pauses, but, on the other hand, do not try "seating out the client" to see who can be the winner. A loud and overbearing manner is exceedingly irritating and makes Indians feel subservient, and this will cause them to shut you out as they clam up and remain quiet. (p. 236)

As discussed in the paragraphs above, understanding simple variations in the physicality of speech can allow us to have a greater understanding when conversing with others from around the world. The intonation and rates of speech have such important meaning in com-munication. For this reason, many people get themselves in trouble when trying to have an important conversation through texting or e-mailing. I myself have been victim to this digital

Figure 7.4 This posture, very common in America, is very offensive in some cultures.

Copyright © Depositphotos/wavebreakmedia.

miscommunication many times. Words themselves are only a small portion of the communication. What's the tone, the facial expression, and the body language in the conversation? These aspects are very difficult to express when texting or e-mailing, but it is through these facets that much of the message is conveyed. Without understanding a culture's nonverbal communications (even if they are very subtle), we may miss an important aspect of the intended message. Choosing not to be offended when someone may stand too close, kiss us on the cheeks, make head movements, or facial expressions while communicating is one step closer to multi-cultural competence.

GESTURES

A person standing in front of you with his or her hands on his or her hips, narrowed eyes, and a foot tapping the ground doesn't need to actually speak any words to communicate anger or frustration. This nonverbal communication, while pretty clear to most Americans, may not be understood by someone from another culture. Bodily movements, whether a nod, facial expression, or hand gesture, can have important implications when communicating. These movements will vary from culture to culture however, and when misunderstood can cause not only a lack of clarity but can also be offensive to local citizens. Watch the following video clip for more examples of physical gestures and their cultural variations.

http://www.youtube.com/watch?v=pxoB6MhmbIg

It's a good idea to know some gestures that may be offensive in other cultures. For example, in many Middle-Eastern and Asian cultures, crossing your ankle on top of your knee exposing the bottom of your foot (as shown in image 7.4) or showing the souls of your feet in any fashion is inappropriate and rude. Again, it's best to do a little research of what gestures or facial expressions are acceptable in any given culture.

INDIRECT VS. DIRECT COMMUNICATION

How is information delivered? Some will come right out and say exactly what they are thinking. Others will *allude* to ideas; the message is delivered but not spoken directly. The following paragraphs will clarify this principle further and include real-world examples.

Reading 7.2

DIRECT VERSUS INDIRECT COMMUNICATION

direct communication—blunt communication that is literal and to the point.

indirect communication—communication that relies upon context and the receiver's ability to draw inferences.

Related to high-versus low-context communication is *direct versus indirect communication*. Most people know that **direct communication** is literal and assertive communication. It is related to low-context communication in that the message is contained in the language used. **Indirect communication** relies on both context and the receiver's powers of inference. To illustrate the difference between these two forms of communication, let us say that someone wants a window closed. Direct speech would say, "Close the window." Indirect speech would say, "Are you cold?" Brown and Levinson (1978) indicated that indirect speech acts are used because they convey a degree of politeness in communication.

Jeffrey Mio, Lori Barker, and Melanie M. Domenech Rodriguez, from "Cultural Differences in Communication," *Multicultural Psychology, 4th ed.*, pp. 117-119. Copyright © 2016 by Oxford University Press. Reprinted with permission.

As such, they are universal.

A student of ours resonated to both indirect communication and high-context communication. She related this rather amusing anecdote to us:

> I come from a culture that values indirectness. I remember when I was getting married; it is customary for the bride to look sad and depressed. She should let her family feel that she is not happy leaving home. If a bride smiles and shows that she is happy it is an indirect way of saying she does not value her family and she would forget them if she leaves home. I cried and acted so sad. My younger sister however took it a step further; she ran away from home the night before her wedding.
>
> I remember my father huffing and puffing and screaming, "If she does not want to marry we would just cancel it—nobody is forcing her." I laughed so hard secretly because I knew she wanted so badly to get married but she was trying to show that she was a "good girl." I always resented the indirect way of doing things because we always have to refuse things and gifts when it is offered to us for the first time and luckily people would continue to insist. God knows how difficult it was for me when I migrated to the USA. I kept insisting my friends eat more or take something I offered them when they said no. They resented it and thought I had no boundaries.
>
> —Adjoa, 40+-Year-Old Ghanaian Immigrant Woman

Yum (1999) acknowledges that indirect communication may be a universal component of all languages. However, she cites wide cultural variations in preference for direct or indirect communication styles. People in many Asian countries are concerned with saving and giving face. Therefore, it should not be surprising to find that indirect speech is prevalent in Asian countries (Katriel, 1986; Lebra, 1976). Lebra (1976) indicated that this level of indirect communication can be extremely subtle. Lebra reported that a woman communicated discord with her mother-in-law based on slight irregularities found in the mother-in-law's flower arrangement. The table summarizes Yum's comparison of North American and East Asian forms of communication.

After reading this section of the book, one of our students reflected on how she sometimes violated the cooperative principle, engaged in indirect communication, and could have avoided a conflict with a friend of hers:

> This chapter in the book reminded me of the times when I violated the cooperative principle which says we should be honest and communicate effectively. For example, I used to be very indirect with people and never really said how I felt. When my best friend lived with my mom and me for the summer, it became tense because my friend would sleep until 2 pm and be in her pajamas watching TV, while the house was a mess. Mom would then complain to me (although she also gave [my friend] indirect messages) that [we were] lazy and did not pull [our] weight around the house. In turn I would give my friend "subtle" hints that she needed to help around the house. I'd say things like, "Uh! How can this house be such a mess!" or I would go around the house cleaning like crazy and move her things and put them in different spots where they would not be seen. I would even wait for her to take her shoes off so I could put them in the closet when she wasn't looking (that was my form of high context communication).
>
> Eventually, I got tired of giving her all these indirect messages and one day, I finally yelled at her that I wasn't her maid. Needless to say, that made our relationship strained (she had no idea how I felt). If I had learned that I should be honest with her about my feelings (using the quality maxim) and not give her dirty looks or roll my eyes at her or give her the "silent treatment" (that was my paralanguage) when she did something I did not like, I could have avoided the blow up and the strained [relationship] that followed.
>
> —Melanie, 20+-Year-Old Mexican American Woman

COMPARISON BETWEEN NORTH AMERICAN AND EAST ASIAN ORIENTATIONS TO COMMUNICATION PATTERNS

East Asian Orientation	North American Orientation
1. *Process orientation.* Communication is perceived as a process of infinite interpretation	*Outcome orientation.* Communication is perceived as the transference of messages.
2. *Differentiated linguistic codes.* Different linguistic codes are used depending upon persons involved and situations.	*Less differentiated linguistic codes.* Linguistic codes are not as extensively differentiated as in East Asia.
3. *Indirect communication emphasis.* The use of indirect communication is prevalent and accepted as normative.	*Direct communication emphasis.* Direct communication is a norm despite the extensive use of indirect communication.
4. *Receiver-centered.* Meaning is in the interpretation. Emphasis is on listening, sensitivity, and removal of preconception	*Sender-centered.* Meaning is in the messages created by the sender. Emphasis is on how to formulate the best messages, how to improve source credibility, and how to improve delivery skills.

Communication is a fundamental facet of any culture. Being aware of differences in communication styles around the world will enhance our cultural experiences while traveling or working with others who have different methods of interpersonal exchange. We mustn't misinterpret one's socialized style of interaction with an intent to offend as it may only be a difference in cultural norms and customs.

Chapter 8

Culture and Gender

The 2010 Global Gender Gap Report by the World Economic Forum shows that countries with better gender equality have faster-growing, more competitive economies.
—Michelle Bachelet, head of UN Women

Figure 8.1

Copyright © Depositphotos/iphemant.

When we hear the term "opposite sex," most of us have immediate thoughts of either a male or a female, but are men and women opposite of each other or complimentary? There are unarguable biological differences between men and women. With few exceptions, female bodies give birth and breastfeed, males produce sperm that can fertilize a woman's egg. These are facts, and no amount of debate can change this reality. Still, these biological functions are less opposing, and more complimentary. Culture is to blame for emphasizing the differences and creating ideologies that support gender stereotypes (Krum Krumov and Knud S. Larsen, 2013). Let's clarify differences between the terms *sex* and *gender*.

Sex refers to the physical characteristics and differences between men and women. **Sex roles** are used to describe the behaviors that men and women may engage in that are directly related to their biological differences and the process of reproduction. **Gender** refers to the behaviors that a culture deems appropriate for men and women. **Gender role** is the degree to which a person adopts the gender specific behaviors ascribed by his or her own culture. And finally, **gender identity** is the degree to which a person has awareness or recognition that he or she adopts a particular gender role.

Are gender roles similar around the world? In what ways have cultures influenced each other on the roles of men and women in society? Read the following paragraphs that discuss this in more detail.

Reading 8.1

CULTURE AND GENDER

Apart from mono-sexual religious groups or cults, men and women live and work together in all cultures of the world. While physiological sexual differences between males and females are universal gender distinctions are the psychological outcomes of culturally determined sexual roles. The common activities of the two genders based on their biological differences and related to reproduction and physiology are called sex roles. The division of labor between the sexes must have emerged out of the need for survival that produced reproductive success when women attended to the needs of children and men worked as providers of shelter and food. Recently men in the United States and Europe are taking on more child caring roles, however, only women can breast feed their babies. On the other hand, gender roles are rapidly evolving and perhaps some will think changing to the point of absurdity. For example, ABC News in December 13th, 2011, reported that 5 million men in the U.S. are now "stay at home Dads" who care for children and other house duties while the wives go to work (Elliot & Francis, 2011).

The rapid social changes in some parts of the world have profoundly affected gender roles in contemporary societies. Men and women have both had to

Krum Krumov and Knud S. Larsen, from "Culture, Sex and Gender," *Cross-Cultural Psychology: Why Culture Matters*, pp. 289-293. Copyright © 2013 by Information Age Publishing. Reprinted with permission.

adapt to gender changes as society has created new role expectations and therefore also stereotypes. Many of these changes have justly benefitted females whose lives have historically been blighted by discrimination. In their eagerness to convince society of the reality and permanence of these changes new stereotypes of the "aggressive female" have emerged that have become mildly laughable. In some television programs in the U.S. we often see physically small women pushing around much larger males showing a masculine toughness that is not emerging clearly from the obvious physical and corresponding psychological differences. In any event when speaking of gender differences we are not speaking of biological sex, but rather of the culturally based behaviors and feelings associated with the social perceptions of gender. While we have much in common as human beings males and females also differ. However, these differences are largely culturally based constructions that have evolved over the course of the history.

SEX ROLES, GENDER STEREOTYPES, AND CULTURE

The biological differences between the sexes are assuredly the basis for the evolution of the division of labor and corresponding sex roles. Sex roles are ubiquitous in all societies and define what men and women are permitted to do and how they are expected to behave. In more rigid traditional societies sex roles also define what the genders should or must do as part of daily interactions. Women are obviously the only sex to give birth and breast feed babies. Nevertheless with the advent of formula baby food, men are taking on feeding responsibilities in some societies. Having noted that exception the genders, however, because of their biological differences may be uniquely placed to perform complementary gender related tasks in child care. However, both sexes can perform many of the same home and work related tasks. Nevertheless women take on most of the obligations related to child care in many societies, and in the modern world where women also work they hold up more than "half" of the heavens to expand on the quotation of Mao.

Sex role theory might also explain ubiquitous gender differences in the expression of emotions. A comparative study of 37 cultures found the same general pattern of gender based emotional expression in both Western and non-Western societies. Typically men express more anger when aroused whereas women tended to express more fear or sadness compared to males (Fischer, Rodriquez Mosquera, van Vianen, & Manstead, 2004). These differences are consistent with the higher level of aggression expected of men and boys, whereas girls and women are expected to be more compassionate. The research also shows that females express emotions more openly than men except in the case of anger. Women seek to foster care-taking and affiliation and are therefore more likely to express feelings of love, sympathy, guilt, and happiness, whereas men do so to a lesser extent for fear of being vulnerable (Brody & Hall, 1993). Men in traditional cultures seek to restore honor when they have been shamed by aggressive or retaliatory behavior, whereas women will react to shame by submissive behavior (Abu-Lughod, 1986).

Culture encourages over time gender based stereotypes that have produced unique social roles. A common finding in Western cultures is the perception of females as weaker, more emotional and more compliant. Males, on the other hand, are typically viewed as assertive, more dominant and independent. The masculine traits produce in men a greater willingness to confront danger and seek adventure that is the basis of the human migration story. The most important study done on gender stereotypes was carried out by Williams and Best (1990a). They submitted a 300-item adjective check list to respondents in twenty-seven countries from the major regions of Europe, Africa, Asia and North and South America. The respondents were asked in a forced choice situation whether the adjective was more descriptive of males or females.

The results showed large differences in all countries surveyed in the perception of what men and women were like. However, even more importantly research supported a broad consensus between countries and cultures on gender stereotypes. Adjectives like active, adventurous and aggressive were associated with males; and affected, affectionate and anxious with females. The consensus in gender stereotypes support these concepts as universal psychological constructs present in all societies. However, some cultural differences were reported. A factor analysis found three meaningful factors labeled favorability, activity and strength. The first factor represented an overall evaluation of the two sexes. While there were no overall differences in male or female favorability in combining scores from all countries, the male stereotype was found to be more favorable in Japan and South Africa, whereas the female stereotype was more favorable in Italy and Peru. From the study it is not clear what cultural or historical factors were responsible for these favorability results. However, on the factor of action orientation males were considered significantly more active. On the third factor of strength there was again a very large mean difference with males scoring higher on the stereotype of being stronger. We can conclude that males and females are within countries attributed very different gender stereotypes and the results showed a remarkable similarity in how these gender distinctions are maintained across cultures.

The extent of the pan-cultural agreement on gender stereotypes is so large that some researchers have suggested that they are the equivalent of psychological universals accepted practically in all societies and by both sexes (Berry, Poortinga, Segall, & Dasen, 1992). Such universal stereotypes lead logically to a consideration of an evolutionary basis that originated in anatomical differences and the subsequent historical division of labor. Reproductive success demanded a division of labor, and those of our ancestors who adapted had an evolutionary advantage in survival. Over the eons of time since early human societies these stereotypes have become a part of cultural history internalized for many people.

The sharpness of the gender differentiation depends on cultural values (Hofstede, 1980). Countries that are conservative with hierarchical social structures and with lower socioeconomic development and where education is valued less for women also display more significant demarcation between the sexes. On the other hand, countries that value egalitarianism as an ideology, social harmony and less traditional sex role orientation, have lower levels of strict gender stereotypical distinctions. When rescoring the Adjective Check List according the BIG Five Model of Personality males were seen as having higher scores on all traits except agreeableness where females scored higher (Williams, Satterwhite, & Best, 1999).

These stereotypes are incorporated at a very early time and Williams and Best found gender stereotypes also present in childhood. Gender stereotypes existed in children in all cultures and were virtually similar to those found for the adult sample. The results suggest that children are inculcated at a very early time in gender stereotypes, in nursery schools, in the home and in other social institutions. Children's stories and the media also play a role in producing such broad agreement on female and male gender characteristics. The fact that there is cross-cultural agreement in children's gender stereotypes support the universal nature of these conceptions and the long evolutionary roots of gender based differences. Nevertheless the role of culture in reinforcing sex roles is supported by the research of Albert and Porter (1986) who reported that gender stereotyping become more prevalent with the increased age of children. Others researchers have emphasized the important role of the media in socializing children in gender stereotypes and with the mass media in the past often showing manifestly demeaning stereotypical images of women (Fejes, 1992). However, since the media in the U.S. and Western Europe were confronted by the women's movement the most blatant and offensive stereotypes have been removed. Of course, culture is persistent and some stereotypes still exist in the modern world.

As noted these stereotypic conceptualizations reflect a genetically based physical reality. However, culture plays a role by socializing gender-related practices that evolved over historical time into a sex role ideology that keep gender expectations rigid even when they do not make sense in the modern world. In the new globalized world of computers women can perform the same work related tasks as men. Women should not be delimited in modern times by a culturally based sex role ideology that grew out of the need for survival in the early history of humanity and the division of labor that placed females in the home. Today women are approaching equity and equality in many areas in the United States and Western Europe and, for example, in the universities women are in some cases out-competing their male counter parts. This independence in females has led to new relationships between the genders and today only half of adults in the United States get married. What the outcome is for family life is difficult to estimate in the intermediate or long-term future.

GENDER SOCIALIZATION AND CHARACTERISTICS

Our role as a male or female is strongly socialized in most cultures. When a woman is expecting a baby, one of the most exciting and anticipated announcements is whether the child is a girl or a boy. There are even special events surrounding the announcement of the biological sex of the child such as cakes that are cut to reveal a pink or blue center, pink or blue balloons released, and songs written and sung, as well as many other clever ways to reveal the big news. Why is this piece of information so important? Most people understand that our gender (whether we want it to or not) greatly affects who we are and what path our life will take.

Watch the following video to see just how strong this socialization of gender can be.

http://www.youtube.com/watch?v=-VqsbvG40Ww

According to the video, by about the age of two, most children understand whether they are a boy or a girl. At about the age of four, most children understand how they should behave based on their biological sex. Williams and Best (1982), who conducted cross-cultural research on gender, summarized the socialization of children in the following excerpt.

> Having found that adults hold stereotypic beliefs about characteristics associated with men and women, we naturally wondered how early in life young children begin to associate different characteristics with the two gender groups. We explored this question in a study of five-year-old-and eight-year-old middle class children in 25 countries. The results indicated that the five-year-old children in all countries showed at least a beginning knowledge of adult stereotypes (Lonner and Malpass 1994).

Williams and Best went on to explain that the greater the differences in male and female gender roles within a culture, the earlier the children were aware of them. For example, in Pakistan they found that children were aware of, and beginning to practice gender roles at earlier ages than children from cultures where the male and female roles were less pronounced.

Gender socialization has been a concern to some members of society because they fear that a child will be "stuck" within this gender role and unable to develop and expand as an individual with these social limitations. Imagine a young boy who loves to play with dolls, wear dresses, and have long hair. His life will NOT be simple when others around him make mention of this behavior as inappropriate. This may also cause concern for the parents that their son may not fit in with peers and suffer negative consequences from the reactions of others.

When one exhibits any gender characteristics that are opposite of one's assigned gender behaviors, it may raise questions about sexual orientation, which causes further stereotypes and biases from others. Males possessing feminine characteristics or females showing more masculine characteristics in a perfect world shouldn't cause

Figure 8.2 By the age of two, most children know whether they are a boy or a girl. By the age of four, most children begin to understand gender roles.

any problems at all. Unfortunately, because of strong socialization efforts within a society and the pressure felt to conform to a specific gender role, it may very well become a traumatic situation accompanied by shame and doubt.

Some parents are SO concerned about gender role limitations that they will take drastic measures to combat it. Watch the following video and ask yourself what the social ramifications are in this situation.

http://abcnews.go.com/GMA/video/parents-gender-child-fight-back-13713224

Some students think this is "tragic" or "unfair" while others applaud their efforts. What is your perception? Would this be a helpful solution? In our culture, this would not be able to go on very long (and it didn't in the end). Do you see this as a positive or negative parenting decision?

PSYCHOLOGICAL CHARACTERISTICS OF MALES AND FEMALES

Another very popular study was done by Williams and Best (1990) on male and female-associated characteristics. They came up with 300 adjectives and asked respondents around the world whether these adjectives would best describe a male or female. I was quite surprised to see that MOST people around the world described the specific male and female attributes in much the same way. For example, most of the research participants thought that reckless, obnoxious, adventurous, arrogant, confident, and courageous were more male-related traits. Women on the other hand, were thought by most to be patient, gentle, submissive, fearful, complicated, and emotional. To summarize this particular study, Williams and Best found that in all countries without exception, the characteristics associated with men were *stronger* and *more active* than those associated with women. In some countries, male stereotypes were more favorable overall, and in others, the traits associated with females were more favorable.

We can see our own culture's views on psychological differences between men and women in television programs and movies. In some popular TV shows for example, (*Everybody Loves Raymond* and *King of Queens* come to mind) the husband and father of the family is portrayed as clueless and un-attentive while the wife and mother is overwhelmed and frustrated by having to take care of important day-to-day household activities. This same scenario can be seen in almost every situation comedy that has a married couple with or without children. The man in the relationship can't possibly survive without the woman to guide and direct his every move. Although this may be changing a bit due to some controversy surrounding it, it still appears to be unfavorable toward men as far as being a successful support system within the home as well as being portrayed as the gender that is without emotion. The female is associated with being overbearing and solely responsible for organizing daily activities and keeping the household running.

Figure 8.3 By a young age, we are taught how we should think and behave as a male or female.

Copyright © Depositphotos/Yasna TenDP.

CROSS-CULTURAL DIFFERENCES IN GENDER ROLES

PATRIARCHAL VS. MATRIARCHAL SOCIETIES

From studies conducted on gender, we have determined (with a few exceptions in cultures that promote a higher level of gender equality) that the gender roles of men and women tend to be similar around the world. It can be a shock to many as they learn of societies that differ significantly from the more common patriarchal society. A **patriarchal family** is a nuclear family consisting of a male head-of-household and female counterpart with a child or two, all living together under the same roof. Men tend to be the main contributors to household income, and women usually stay home and care for the children and household. We have seen that these roles are rapidly changing; however, this nuclear family and patriarchal society have been a strong part of our culture as well as many others around the world.

Figure 8.4 The gender roles of the Mosuo women living in Yunnan, China, differ from many other cultures.

There are cultures (while it may be uncommon) that have what is called a **matriarchal society**, where the head of the household is female and mother of the family. Some anthropologists use this term to define societies in which women have equal rights as well as families or tribes headed by mothers or grandmothers. Watch the following video to learn more about this type of society in a small village in China.

https://www.youtube.com/watch?v=eoTrARDa8BU

Allowing a woman at the young age of 13 to make mature decisions about her sexual life and her future as seen in this video clip, may be cause for great concern in many cultures. How do you feel about this lifestyle? Do you believe that a matriarchal society would change the beliefs many have around the world of male and female capabilities? Why are there misconceptions about their lifestyle by outsiders?

WHAT DOES THIS MEAN TO ME?

What are your personal ideas about gender roles? How do you think and behave when associating with males and females? Do you follow gender roles that were taught at a young age? Did your parents have traditional male and female roles? Were you raised in a home with a single parent? If so, how do you think this affected you and your ideas about gender characteristics? Do you believe there are innate, psychological differences between males and females? Why is it important to be aware of culture and socialization when discussing male and female relationships? Become aware of your own thoughts on gender and gender roles and how this affects who you are.

MATE PREFERENCES

How do we choose our mates? What characteristics do we desire and why? It's been assumed that what we desire in a mate is culture bound; for example, people in North America will desire different characteristics than those in Asia or Africa. David M. Buss, a professor of psychology and author of *Human Mating Strategies*, studied 37 different cultures on six continents and five islands on mate preferences. While he did find some differences, he and his team also found universal preferences, as well. "When we analyzed the data for each of the 37 cultures, we found that people in nearly every culture agreed about which were the top few most desirable characteristics" (Lonner and Malpass 1994).

There were two different aspects of the research. The first was to rate thirteen characteristics by importance, the second instrument was to request the research subjects to rank each characteristic from "1," the most desirable, to "13," the least desirable. Both men and women wanted a mate who was kind and understanding, intelligent, had an exciting personality, and who was healthy. This summarized the "ranking," but there were also universal preferences rated that included mutual attraction—love, emotionally stable and mature, dependable character, good health, and pleasing disposition.

Many scientists believed that "love" is just important to those in the Western part of the world. Through these particular studies however, it was found that love and mutual attraction is just as important to someone in Asia and Africa as they are to people on the Western side of the world. David Buss and colleagues found through their research that mate preferences and the idea of mutual love is not as culture bound as originally thought.

CULTURAL DIFFERENCES IN MATE PREFERENCES

While researchers were surprised to find so many similarities in mate preferences, there were also a few characteristics that had significant *differences* between cultures. Chastity (or the lack of previous sexual intercourse) was found to have the greatest variance. In some cultures such as the Netherlands, there were respondents that found the lack of previous sexual relationships undesirable. In China on the other hand, marrying a non-virgin was out of the question. Other cultures that value chastity are India, Iran, and Taiwan. Sweden and Norway were among those cultures that cared the least about chastity. In NO cultures was virginity MORE important to women than it was to men. In two-thirds of the cultures studied, men valued chastity in marriage partners more than women. Other traits in a companion that were important in some cultures and meant nothing in others, were such things as being neat, a good housekeeper, and religious. Not surprisingly, mates who are religious, were important in cultures such as Iran and Nigeria but less valued in Great Britain and Australia (Lonner and Malpass 1994).

PREFERENCES SPECIFIC TO WOMEN AND MEN

Gender roles are evident in what women value in men. It was found that most women value good financial prospects, good earning capacity, ambitiousness, industriousness, and social status more than men. Women value resources. They want to know that their spouse will be able to take care of them and their offspring. Women across all cultures tended to be more "choosy" than men in selecting a mate. Women have the evolutionary need to be able to care for their children.

Men showed a stronger preference than women in two areas. Men preferred women who were younger than they were and were more interested in physical attractiveness. What makes the mate attractive differs among cultures however. "Beauty is in the eye of the beholder" is a phrase that works here. How much younger men preferred their mate to be depends on the culture in which they were raised. In polygamous cultures, men preferred wives much younger than they were. Women also preferred men who were older than they were and again, this is believed to be because older men may have more resources. It was also shown that marriage dissolution is prevalent worldwide when there is infertility, infidelity, and a man's failure to provide economically.

PHYSICAL PREFERENCES

If there are characteristics in another person that are desired universally, there must certainly be physical preferences as well, and indeed there are! Research shows that people across cultures see clear and supple skin, absence of wrinkles, lustrous hair, full lips, clear eyes, good health, regular features, and other signs of youth and health as attractive (Lonner and Malpass 1994).

What is perceived as attractive is definitely dependent on one's cultural upbringing. In many places around the world, a woman who is bigger in size is a sign of beauty, strength, and potential reproduction. In some places, the bigger a man can get physically, the more attractive he becomes to the female because it states indirectly that he has plenty to eat and can therefore, provide well for a family. As you can see, this is quite different from America where body size and being thin is extremely important, and is one of the reasons that the U.S. is the home to a culture-bound syndrome called anorexia, which we will discuss in a later chapter.

Being born a male or a female in any society carries with it a very important facet of one's life. Should your gender define who you are and what you will do in your life? Just as with any other topic in psychology and culture, the way we view gender and gender roles depends on the way we were socialized as a child from a young age. Men and women are different in many ways and sadly, these differences have created inequality in the minds of many. Gender differences are not opposing, like the term "opposite sex" would imply, but complimentary. Each individual, in spite of gender, is, and should be treated as, an important and unique part of the greater whole.

Chapter 9

Culture and Mental Health

The mad man thinks the rest of the world is crazy.
—Publilius Syrus (First Century B.C.E.)

Figure 9.1

Copyright © Depositphotos/kwest.

PERSPECTIVES ON MENTAL HEALTH

Culture plays a major role in mental health in how behavior symptoms are manifested, in the way mental disorders are communicated, and even whether patients will seek assistance (Eshun and Gurung 2009). One of the obstacles when studying and comparing mental disorders around the world is the definition of "abnormal." What criteria is used to determine if one is mentally ill? Culture defines what's normal or abnormal. If a person cannot function with day-to-day activities that are important in that culture, then it may be considered an "abnormality."

129

By definition, a **mental disorder** is a clinically significant behavioral and psychological syndrome or pattern that occurs in an individual and that is associated with present distress or disability or with a significantly increased risk of suffering death, pain, disability, or an important loss of freedom (*DSM-IV*, p. xxi). While there's a definition of a mental disorder, there are varying cultural perspectives on these psychological disturbances which can make recognizing and diagnosing disorders challenging. As discussed in Chapter 2, there are two basic perspectives when researching phenomena cross-culturally. Shiraev and Levy (2013) explain these views in relation to mental illness in the paragraphs below.

Human beings develop ideas, establish behavioral norms, and learn emotional responses according to a set of cultural prescriptions. Therefore, people from different cultural settings should understand psychological disorders differently, and the differences should be significant. This view is called the **relativist perspective** on psychopathology because it puts psychological phenomena in a relative perspective.

Despite cultural differences, people have a great number of similar features, including attitudes, values, and behavioral responses. Therefore, the overall understanding of mental disorders ought to be universal. This view is called the **universalist perspective** on psychopathology because it suggests the existence of absolute, invariable symptoms of psychopathology across cultures.

CULTURE BOUND SYNDROMES

With varying perspectives on mental health issues around the world, how then would organizations such as the World Health Organization (WHO) or manuals such as the *International Classification of Diseases* (*ICD*) or the *Diagnostic and Statistical Manual of Mental Disorders* (*DSM-5*) be able to classify these variances in order to accommodate the opposing views on abnormalities? There is a solution to this challenge in addition to research findings on culture-bound syndromes and similarities on illnesses found worldwide in the following paragraphs from Shiraev and Levy (2013) in their text *Cross-Cultural Psychology*.

Reading 9.1

CENTRAL AND PERIPHERAL SYMPTOMS: AN OUTCOME OF THE DEBATE BETWEEN UNIVERSALISTS AND RELATIVISTS

Which view, absolutist or relativist, describes psychological reality with a greater accuracy? While understanding both the relative cultural uniqueness and the universal nature of psychopathology, it is useful to implement an inclusive approach to psychopathology that combines the two previously described viewpoints. That is, major features of psychopathology—abnormality, maladaptiveness, and distress—should be considered universal. However, these features manifest by individuals in specific environmental, social, and cultural contexts. Each disorder, therefore, can manifest as follows:

- A set of **central symptoms** that can be observed in practically all world populations and

- A set of peripheral symptoms that are culture specific.

For example, central symptoms for a case of a major depressive episode, such as dysphoria, loss of energy, tension, and ideas of insufficiency, could be seen cross-culturally as

1. caused by biochemical factors;

2. a bodily syndrome manifested in the form of fatigue, lack of concentration, and various pains; and

3. psychological complaints such the inability to take pleasure in previously enjoyable activities.

Peripheral (culture-specific) signs of this illness vary. Thus, many Canadian patients may display guilty feelings. Some of them would report preoccupations with suicid-

Eric B. Shiraev and David A. Levy, from "Psychological Disorders," *Cross-Cultural Psychology: Critical Thinking and Contemporary Applications*, pp. 220-224. Copyright © 2013 by Taylor & Francis Group. Reprinted with permission.

al thoughts. Most patients from Taiwan will be unlikely to report guilty feelings. Guilt, shame, bodily pain, or behavioral disturbance may be the dominant presentation, depending on one's learned expectation of what is relevant to his or her particular illness (Turner. 1997).

CULTURE-BOUND SYNDROMES

Culture-bound syndromes comprise a set of psychological phenomena of particular interest to psychologists. The eclectic nature of the category makes it hard to define precisely. It has even invited much dispute over the best definition for it. *DSM-IV* defines a culture-bound syndrome as recurrent, locality-specific patterns of aberrant behavior, and troubling experience that may or may not be linked to a particular *DSM-IV* diagnostic category. Many of these patterns are indigenously viewed as "illnesses." or at least afflictions, and most have local names.

Culture-bound syndromes do not have a one-to-one correspondence with a disorder recognized by "mainstream" systems. Most of these syndromes were initially reported as confined to a particular culture or set of related or geographically proximal cultures. At least seven broad categories can be differentiated among phenomena often described as culture-bound syndromes:

1. An apparent set of psychopathological symptoms, not attributable to an identifiable organic cause, which is recognized as an illness in a particular cultural group, but does not fall into the illness category in the West. *Amok*, a sudden explosion of rage, recognizable in Malaysia, is an example. In London or New York, a person with these symptoms is likely to be described as "having [an] anger-control problem."

2. An apparent set of psychopathological symptoms, not attributable to an identifiable organic cause, which is locally recognized as an illness and which resembles a Western disease category, but which (1) has locally salient features different from the Western disease and (2) lacks some symptoms recognizable in the West. One example is *shenjingshaijo* or neurasthenia in China, which resembles major depressive disorder but has more salient somatic features and often lacks the depressed mood that defines depression in the West.

3. A discrete disease entity not yet recognized by Western professionals. A fine example of this is *kuru*, a progressive psychosis and dementia indigenous to cannibalistic tribes in New Guinea. *Kuru* is now believed to result from an aberrant protein or "prion" that is capable of replicating itself by deforming other proteins in the brain. (A 1997 Nobel Prize was awarded for the elucidation of prions.) *Kuru* has also been compared to a form of Creuzfeldt-Jakob disease and may be equivalent or related to *scrapie*, a disease of sheep, and a form of *encephalopathy* labeled "mad cow disease."

4. An illness, the symptoms of which occur in many cultural settings: however, it is only elaborated as an illness in one or a few cultural settings. An example is *koro*, the fear of retracting genitalia, which may sometimes have a physiological-anatomical reality and appears to occur as a delusion or phobia in several cultural groups.

5. Culturally accepted explanatory mechanisms or idioms of illness, which do not match Western idioms of distress and, in a Western setting, might indicate culturally inappropriate thinking and perhaps delusions or hallucinations. Examples of this include witchcraft, *rootwork* (in Caribbean), or the *evil eye* (common in Mediterranean and Latin American traditions).

6. A state or set of behaviors, often including trance or possession states: hearing, seeing, and/or communicating with the dead or spirits or feeling that one has "lost one's soul" from grief or fright. These may or may not be seen as pathological within their native cultural framework but, if not recognized as culturally appropriate could indicate psychosis, delusions, or hallucinations in a Western setting.

7. A syndrome allegedly occurring in a given cultural setting, which does not in fact exist but may be reported to the professional. A possible example is *windigo* (in Algonkian Indians), a syndrome of cannibal obsessions, the existence of which is questionable (Marano, 1985); this allegation, however, may be used to justify the expulsion or execution of a tribal outcast in a manner similar to the use of witchcraft allegations (see Table).

TABLE - SPECIFIC CULTURE-BOUND SYNDROMES

These are recurrent, locally specific patterns of atypical behavior and troubling experiences that may or may not be linked to a particular *DSM-IV* diagnostic category (*DSM-IV*, p. 844). Culture-bound syndromes are generally limited to specific societies or areas and indicate repetitive and troubling sets of experiences and observations. Consider examples of some culture-bound disorders. Try to find both central and peripheral symptoms in each syndrome.

Amok. Known in Malaysia; similar patterns may occur elsewhere. Amok is a sudden rage in which an otherwise normal person goes berserk, sometimes hurting those in his path. Brooding is followed by a violent outburst; it is often precipitated by a slight or insult. The symptoms seem to be prevalent among men. It was well known to the British colonial rulers of Malaysia and has therefore passed into the English language: "running amok." To this day, cases of amok are reported in Malaysian newspapers (Osborne, 2001).

Ataque de nervios. Also known as "attack of nerves." Common in Latin America and Mediterranean groups. Symptoms include uncontrollable shouting, attacks of crying, trembling, heat in the chest rising to the head, and verbal or physical aggression. Ataque de nervios frequently occurs as a result of not only a stressful family event, especially the death of a relative, but also a divorce or fight with a family member. Studies of *ataque de nervios* revealed that 26 percent of people who suffer from this condition had a strong risk factor for other psychiatric disorders. More than 80 percent of these people have symptoms associated with anxiety, mood, suicidal; psychotic, or substance use dysfunctions (Tolin et al., 2007).

Bilis, colera, or muina. Part of a general Latin American idiom of distress and explanation of physical or mental illness as a result of extreme emotion that upsets the humors (described in terms of hot and cold). Other symptoms include tension, headache, trembling, screaming, and so on. Bilis and colera specifically implicate anger in the cause of illness. In Korea, similar symptoms are labeled *Hwa-byung* or *wool-hwa-bung*, or the "anger syndrome." Symptoms are attributed to suppression of anger and include insomnia, fatigue, panic, fear of impending death, indigestion, anorexia, palpitations, generalized aches and pains, and a feeling of a mass in the epigastrium.

Brain fag. Known in West Africa. Sometimes labeled "brain tiredness," this is a mental and physical reaction to the challenges of schooling, a condition experienced primarily by male high school or university students. Symptoms include difficulties in concentrating, remembering, and thinking. Students often state that their brains are "fatigued." Additional symptoms center around the head and neck and include pain, pressure, tightness, blurring of vision, heat, or burning. "Brain tiredness" or fatigue from "too much thinking" is an idiom of distress in many cultures. The symptoms resemble anxiety, depressive, or somatoform disorders in *DSM-IV*.

Dhat. Occurs in India, similar conditions are described in Sri Lanka and China too. This syndrome is characterized by excessive concern about loss of semen through excessive sexual activity or in the urine. Dhat syndrome presents with weakness, depression, and sexual problems and symptoms, such as palpitations, in a rather nonspecific form; similar to *jiryan* (also in India), *sukrapremeha* (in Sri Lanka), and *shenkui* (in China). Symptoms are attributed to excessive semen loss from frequent intercourse, masturbation, nocturnal emission, or urine. Excessive semen loss is feared because it represents the loss of one's vital essence and can thereby be life threatening.

Falling out. Recognized in Southern United States, and "blacking out," as known in the Caribbean. Symptoms: sudden collapse; loss of sight even though eyes remain open. The person usually hears and understands what is occurring around him but feels powerless to move. These symptoms are labeled *obmorok* in Russian culture. May correspond to conversion disorder or dissociative disorder (*DSM-IV*).

Frigophobia. There is a condition that the Chinese call *weihanzheng*, or "fear of being cold." Patients bundle up in the steamy heat, wearing wool hats and gloves. Frigophobia seems to stem from Chinese cultural beliefs about the spiritual qualities of heat and cold; these symptoms are described primarily in the Chinese population of Singapore.

Ghost sickness. Reported in people from Native American Indian. Symptoms include preoccupations with death and the dead, bad dreams, fainting, appetite loss, fear, witchcraft, hallucinations, a sense of suffocation, confusion, and so on.

Koro. Is known to people of Chinese ethnicity in Malaysia; related conditions are described in some other parts of East Asia. Main symptom: People experience sudden and intense anxiety that sexual organs will recede into body and cause death.

(continued)

Latah. Occurs in Malaysia, Indonesia, Thailand, and Japan. Symptoms include hypersensitivity to sudden fright, often with nonsense mimicking of others, and trancelike behavior. Over time, the person with these symptoms becomes so sensitive that trances can be triggered by a falling coconut. Latahs (people who display the symptoms of latah) tend to blurt out offensive phrases, much like sufferers of Tourette's syndrome. (Indeed, Georges Gilles de la Tourette, the French discoverer of the syndrome in the 1880s, explicitly compared it to latah.) *Latahs* also often mimic the actions of people around them or obey commands, including requests to take off their clothes. Afterward, people often claim to have no memory of what they said or did.

Locura. Incidents are known in the United States and Latin America. Symptoms include incoherence, agitation, auditory and visual hallucinations, inability to follow rules of social interaction, unpredictability, and possible violence.

Mai de ojo ("evil eye"). Known in people from the Mediterranean and elsewhere. Sufferers, mostly children, are believed to be under the influence of an "evil eye," causing fitful sleep, crying, sickness, and fever.

Pibloktoq. Known in people from the Arctic and sub-Arctic Inuit communities, such as Greenland Eskimos. The syndrome is found throughout the Arctic with local names. Symptoms include extreme excitement, physical violence, verbal abuse, convulsions, and short coma During the attack, the individual may tear off his clothing, break furniture, shout obscenities, eat feces, flee from protective shelters, or perform other irrational or dangerous acts. The individual may be withdrawn or mildly irritable for a period of hours or days before the attack and will typically report complete amnesia of the attack.

Qi-gong. Known in China. A short episode of symptoms, such as auditory and visual hallucinations, occurs after engaging in Chinese folk practice of qi-gong, or "exercise of vital energy," which resembles meditation (Lim & Lin, 1996). In the United States, reports about persistent hallucinations are likely to suggest schizophrenia or schizophreniform disorder.

Rootwork. Symptoms are known in the Southern United States and the Caribbean. They include anxiety, such as fear of poisoning or death, ascribed to those individuals who put "roots," "spells," or "hexes" on others.

Sin-byung. Known in Korea. This is the syndrome of anxiety and bodily complaints followed by dissociation and possession by ancestral spirits. The syndrome is characterized by general weakness, dizziness, fear, loss of appetite, insomnia, and gastrointestinal problems.

The sore neck syndrome. This is a syndrome observed in Khmer refugees. The main feature involves a fear that blood and wind pressures will cause vessels in the neck area to burst. Additional symptoms include palpitations, shortness of breath, panicking, headache, blurry vision, a buzzing in the ear, dizziness, and trembling.

Spell. Symptoms are described by some individuals in the Southern United States and elsewhere in the world. This is a trance in which individuals communicate with deceased relatives or spirits. At times this trance is associated with brief periods of personality change. This is not considered psychopathological in the folk tradition; however, this phenomenon is often labeled "psychotic episodes" in Western clinical settings.

Susto. Found in Latin American groups in the United States and labeled "fright" or "soul loss" among some people from the Caribbean. Symptoms are tied to a frightening event that makes the soul leave the body, causing unhappiness and sickness.

Taijinkyofusho. In Japan, it is an intense fear that one's body, body parts, or bodily functions are displeasing, embarrassing, or offensive to other people in appearance, odor, facial expressions, or movements. This malady is included in the official Japanese classification of mental disorders. The symptoms are perhaps similar, in some respect, to social phobia (*DSM-IV*).

Zar. Known in Ethiopia, Somalia, Egypt, Sudan, Iran, and elsewhere in North Africa and the Middle East. This is the belief in possession by a spirit, causing shouting, laughing, head banging, singing, or weeping. Individuals may show apathy and withdrawal, refusing to eat or carry out daily tasks, or may develop a long-term relationship with the possessing spirit. Such behavior is not necessarily considered pathological in local settings.

Debates over culture-bound syndromes often revolve around confusions or conflations among these different categories. Many so-called culture-bound syndromes actually occur in many unrelated cultures, or they appear to be merely locally flavored varieties of illnesses found elsewhere. This fact is especially interesting because it shows that culture-bound syndromes could be viewed as an accentuation of the universal trends. Specific cultures construe certain behaviors as syndromes of psychopathology, name them disorders, and treat them as illnesses. Some are not so much actual illnesses as explanatory mechanisms, such as beliefs in witchcraft or humoral imbalances (a shift in the balance of some "bodily liquids"). So-called "male pregnancy symptoms"—vomiting, fatigue, toothache, and food cravings during a partner's pregnancy were studied in On Wogeo, an island off the coast of New Guinea, the Garifuna (or Black Carib) of Central America, the Bimin-Kuskusmin of Papua New Guinea (Munroe, 2010). Are these special culture-bound syndromes or just local variations of sympathy pain, which many of us can experience? The concept of culture-bound syndromes is therefore useful insofar as it brings culture (religion and ethnic identity in particular) to the attention of psychiatrists and psychologists trained in a different cultural tradition (Simons & Hughes, 1985).

Figure 9.2 Some conditions are rarely seen outside of a particular culture. Anorexia nervosa was "culture bound" in America when it was first recognized as a disorder.

Copyright © Depositphotos/Sergo221972.

Does the United States have a "culture-bound syndrome?" Because of our cultural views on a small and thin body size, young girls started to develop eating disorders. It began with anorexia nervosa and progressed to other disorders, such as bulimia and body dysmorphic disorder. While most of those who suffer are females, boys (and sometimes grown men) are now susceptible to these issues as well. Because of globalization through exposure to movies and magazines highlighting American norms, other countries are seeing more of these eating disorders.

CULTURAL SIMILARITIES AND DIFFERENCES IN PSYCHOPATHOLOGY

Many disorders have been found to have almost identical symptoms around the world. Among these mental ailments are those of Alzheimer's, dementia, Parkinson's disease, mental retardation, schizophrenia, and autism (Shiraev and Levy 2013). These disorders have more of a biological base, so seeing global similarities is not surprising since we are all human and we have the same basic physical functions. Postpartum depression for women, in spite of differing cultural backgrounds, tends to have the same characteristics physically and mentally. Another interesting similarity found worldwide was that caring for a family member with mental illness was associated with negative stigmas and many times, associated with guilt, shame, and hopelessness.

Reading 9.2

CULTURE AND DIAGNOSIS

Diagnostic and Statistical Manual of Mental Disorders—the primary reference manual used in all mental health fields to classify mental disorders. Published by the American Psychiatric Association, this manual is currently in its fifth edition (2013).

We cannot have a discussion about culture and the **diagnosis of mental disorders** without talking about the *Diagnostic and Statistical Manual of Mental Disorders* (*DSM*). The *DSM* is the primary manual used by health and mental health professionals in the United States to diagnose mental disorders. The *DSM* has gone through several revisions. The most current version is the *DSM-5* the fifth edition (American Psychiatric Association, 2013).

Although the *DSM* is used in other countries, there are other diagnostic manuals, including one developed by the World Health Organization (WHO, 2007), the *International Statistical Classification of Diseases and Related Health Problems*, currently in its tenth version (*ICD-10*). The *ICD-10* is an international classification system for all diseases and health problems, not just mental disorders. The developers of the *DSM-5* and the *ICD-10* worked closely together, so the two manuals are compatible. Individual countries also have their own diagnostic manuals. For example, in China they use the *Chinese Classification of Mental Disorders*, 3rd edition (*CCMD-3*). The *CCMD-3* is also written to correspond with both the *DSM* and the *ICD*; however, it also includes some cultural variations on the main diagnoses and approximately 40 culture-specific diagnoses. It is published in both Chinese and English (Lee, 2001; Surhone, Tennoe, & Henssonow, 2010).

Jeffrey Mio, Lori Barker, and Melanie M. Domenech Rodriguez, from "Culture and Mental Health," *Multicultural Psychology, 4th ed.*, pp. 283-287. Copyright © 2016 by Oxford University Press. Reprinted with permission.

The World Psychiatric Association (WPA) and WHO conducted a survey of almost 5,000 psychiatrists across 44 countries regarding the cross-cultural utility of diagnostic classification systems like the *DSM* and *ICD* (Reed, Correia, Esparza, Saxena, & Maj, 2011). Most of the participating psychiatrists (70.1%) reported using the *ICD-10*, and most of the remainder (23.0%) the *DSM-IV* (the study was conducted before *DSM-5* came out). A small percentage (5.6%) reported using another system (e.g., the CCMD). The survey also included the question, "The diagnostic system I use is difficult to apply across cultures, or when the patient/service user is of a different cultural or ethnic background from my own." Overall, about 75% of the worldwide participants agreed with this statement. However, when the responses were divided by region, some differences appeared. Nearly 30% of the participants in Latin America, East Asia and Southeast Asia agreed with this statement, while only 10% of those from the United States did so. Many psychiatrists from countries such as Cuba, Russia, China, India, Japan, and France also felt there was a need for classification systems specific to their nations. In other words, a significant number of psychiatrists around the world questioned the applicability of global diagnostic systems like the *DSM* to the patients they serve.

THE DIAGNOSTIC AND STATISTICAL MANUAL OF MENTAL DISORDERS: A CLASSIFICATION SYSTEM

Diagnostic categories in the *DSM* are based on empirical research and focus on behavioral descriptions of symptoms. Specific diagnoses represent clusters of symptoms that typically are seen together and that have some defining feature. A diagnosis is made on the basis of a set of behavioral criteria. If the person exhibits a minimum number of symptoms in the list, then a specific diagnosis is made. For example, major depressive disorder has a list of nine symptoms, including depressed mood, loss of interest or pleasure in usual activities, weight loss, and insomnia. For a diagnosis to be made, the person must experience five or more of these symptoms for at least 2 weeks. By focusing on behavioral manifestations of symptoms, the *DSM* attempts to be neutral. This enables it to be a useful communication tool for people from an array of professional backgrounds (e.g., psychologists, medical doctors, social workers), with different theoretical orientations (e.g., behavioral, psychodynamic, family/systems), in a variety of settings (e.g., hospitals, clinics, private practice; American Psychiatric Association, 2013).

The *DSM-IV* (American Psychiatric Association, 1994) was the first version of the

DSM to systematically include cultural issues. Now, a section on cultural issues is included with each of the diagnostic categories. In addition, there is an "Outline for Cultural Formulation," which is a guide that helps mental health professionals systematically review the client's cultural background, the role of culture in the expression of the client's symptoms, and the role that cultural differences may play in the relationship between the client and the therapist. The outline identifies five areas that the therapist should cover in making a cultural assessment of the client and his or her presenting problems: (a) the cultural identity of the individual; (b) cultural conceptualization of distress, or the factors that influence how the person experiences, understands, and communicates his or her symptoms; (c) psychosocial stressors and cultural features of vulnerability and resilience, including culturally relevant social stressors and available social support; (d) cultural elements of the relationship between the individual and the clinician, including how cultural differences between the client and the therapist may affect the treatment; and (e) overall cultural assessment for diagnosis and care, in which the therapist incorporates all these cultural factors to plan the most appropriate course of treatment (American Psychiatric Association, 2013). The *DSM-5* also includes a structured interview to help clinicians cover each of these areas called the Cultural Formulation Interview (CFI).

The *DSM-5* gives a more detailed description of the second area, cultural concepts of distress. Again, this refers to the ways in which individuals and cultural groups experience, understand, and communicate their problems. The *DSM-5* identifies three types of cultural concepts. The first are *cultural syndromes*, or clusters of symptoms that tend to occur only in specific cultural groups. These used to be referred to as culture-bound syndromes. The second are *cultural idioms* of distress, or specific ways of expressing troubling thoughts, behaviors, and emotions. Finally, are *cultural explanations or perceived causes*. In other words, certain cultural groups may attach unique meanings to symptoms or have particular explanations for the etiology of illness or distress. These cultural concepts typically arise out of local folkways and may or may not correspond to specific *DSM* diagnostic categories. *DSM-5* also includes a Glossary of Cultural Concepts of Distress. We will give some examples of these later in the chapter.

The initial inclusion of cultural issues in *DSM-IV* was a clear step in the right direction, and some see *DSM-5* as even further improvement (e.g., Cummings, 2013; Saville-Smith, 2013). Cummings (2013) sees it as a "vast improvement" in making the *DSM* more inclusive. However, there are those who believed *DSM-IV* did not go far enough (Lopez & Guarnaccia, 2000; Parham, 2002) and, despite more extensive coverage of culture in *DSM-5*, it still has its critics and those who question its utility with diverse cultural groups (Jacob, 2014; Jacob et al., 2013; Reed et al., 2011).

Although the *DSM* strives to be an objective diagnostic tool, research studies repeatedly demonstrate clinician bias in applying diagnostic criteria. Clients reporting the same symptoms are given different diagnoses. Several studies have shown that African Americans are more likely to be diagnosed with schizophrenia and less likely to be diagnosed with a mood disorder, while the opposite is true for non-African Americans (e.g., Adembimpe, 1981; Neighbors, 1997; Trierweiler et al., 2005). In other words, there is a tendency for therapists to give the more serious, chronic, stigmatized diagnosis of schizophrenia to African American clients and a less severe diagnosis, such as major depression, to European American clients.

CULTURE AND THE EXPRESSION OF SYMPTOMS

somatization—the expression of mental disorders through physical disorders.

An accurate diagnosis depends both on the client's ability to describe his or her symptoms and on the clinician's ability to observe and to accurately interpret those symptoms. Culture influences the way in which individuals express the symptoms of various disorders. People from different cultures may have the same disorder but may experience and describe their symptoms in very different ways. The manifestation of symptoms can vary with age, gender, race, ethnicity, and culture.

Let us again use the example of depression. Certain cultures might experience and express more physical symptoms than mood symptoms. This is known as **somatization**, or the expression of psychological symptoms through physical ones. For example, individuals from Latino and Mediterranean cultures may complain of "nerves" or headaches, those from Middle Eastern cultures may complain of problems of the "heart," and Asians may talk about weakness, tiredness, or "imbalance." It is important for the clinician to be aware of such cultural differences in expression to avoid misdiagnosis. For example, some individuals may express a fear of being hexed or bewitched, or may report vivid feelings of being visited by someone who has died. These may be acceptable and understood experiences in some cultures but could be mistaken by a traditional Western therapist for symptoms of psychosis.

In addition, the expression of depressive symptoms can change with age. The symptoms described in *DSM-5* criteria typically describe how depression is experienced by adolescents and adults. Children may have somatic complaints as well as irritability and social withdrawal, and their depression often coexists with other behavioral problems, such as disruptive behavior, hyperactivity, and inattention. In contrast, depressive symptoms in the elderly may include disorientation, memory loss, and distractibility. These must be distinguished from the symptoms of dementia (American Psychiatric Association, 2013).

Chanda relocated to the United States after surviving the horrors of Pol Pot's regime in Cambodia. While living in Cambodia she lost most of the members of her extended family who were either killed by the Khmer Rouge (the ruling party) or from starvation. Chanda was married four times. Her first husband was beaten to death by the Khmer Rouge. Her second husband died of an illness while they were awaiting resettlement in the refugee camp. Her third husband left with another woman, and she separated from her fourth husband. Chanda was pregnant 12 times. She lost six to miscarriages and two died from starvation.

She has four surviving children—one who was the only one to survive the Pol Pot era, the second who was born in a refugee camp, and the last two that were born after she immigrated to the United States. She describes the living conditions on one of the farms she worked in Cambodia:

"When the floods came we had nothing to eat at all. Living there, you know? And from working and over-exhaustion, having nothing to eat. Some months, when there was no rice at all, they would make soup out of rice peel (husk) for us to eat. There were even people who ate their own children. There was a lady who ate her dead baby, too hungry! If you don't believe me, go see for yourself, and you'll see that this village is full of skeletons.... We would walk around looking for food, even one little plant; we left no leaves on it."

Chanda resettled in the United States in 1983. Since then she has suffered continuously from various forms of illness, physical pain, constant coughing, feeling that something was stuck in her throat, allergies, hearing voices, and seeing spirits. Chanda describes going to the hospital where they took X-rays, but the medical people were unable to determine the cause of her problem because nothing showed up in the photos. She says:

"I told them that I had fever and things. As soon as I came down with a fever, it was like 'a hundred ghosts took over my body.' I was sick on that day. Within one hour, it was like I was sick with 10 different illnesses. I would sit there and hear ringing. I told the doctors that this hurt and that hurt, because it really did hurt inside my body. My arm hurt, to this day it hurts where I extend my arm and the pain won't go away. If I don't take painkillers I would 'sleep in tears' every night."

Chanda also experienced spirit visitations. She says these spirits keep telling her things, and she keeps seeing something from another world. Chanda's descriptions of her visitations from spirits caused her to be hospitalized for a week.

(Adapted from Morelli, 2005, pp. 130–134)

Although Chanda may have some physical symptoms as a result of her many years of starvation, we can also see the tendency to somaticize, or to express psychological symptoms as physical ones. We also see some symptoms that the traditional Western doctors diagnosed as psychosis (visitations from spirits), but that may represent a culturally appropriate or acceptable experience.

CULTURAL GROUP DIFFERENCES AND MENTAL HEALTH

prevalence—the current rate of a particular disorder at a given point in time.

incidence—the number of new cases of a disorder diagnosed in a given period of time.

In the field of public health, **prevalence** is defined as the current rate of existing cases of a disorder at a given point in time. An example would be the number of people currently diagnosed with schizophrenia. Another term used quite often when reporting rates of various disorders is **incidence**, which refers to the number of new cases of a disorder that occur during a given period of time, such as the number of people who are diagnosed with schizophrenia this year. **Lifetime incidence** refers to the number of cases of a disorder that occur during one's lifetime. Therefore, if an individual was diagnosed with schizophrenia 2 years ago and continues to suffer from this disorder, that person would be included in the prevalence rate, would not be included in the incidence rate in the past year, but would be included in the lifetime incidence rate.

> **lifetime incidence**—the number of cases of a disorder that occur during one's lifetime.

There is a great deal of interest in comparing the incidence and prevalence rates of disorders in the different ethnic groups. The literature is mixed, with some studies showing lower rates of mental disorders in ethnic minority populations and some showing greater rates, making it difficult to draw conclusions about ethnic group differences and mental disorders. However, the results of a few large epidemiologic studies reveal some trends.

The greatest happiness is to know the source of unhappiness.

—Fyodor Dostoyevsky (1821–1881)

ANXIETY

Symptoms of an anxiety disorder can be universally reported as a persistent worry, fear, or a constant state of apprehensive anticipation—the conditions are maladaptive and cause significant distress in the individual. The *central symptoms* of anxiety would be the "fear" of a situation no matter what the *peripheral symptoms* may be. For example, one could experience bodily symptoms such as heart palpitations, perspiration, nauseous stomach, and fear because of a peripheral symptom such as a fear of spiders or another peripheral and culturally-related fear of being offensive to others as in some Asian cultures (Shiraev and Levy 2013). One aspect of anxiety that is found to be the same across cultures is the relationship between traumatic events and the development of anxiety disorders. Those who experience a negative, life-altering event such as terrorism, torture, natural disasters, or rape all have similar behavioral responses even if cultural backgrounds are different.

DEPRESSION

Often called *Melancholy, or Melancholia*, depressive disorders have reached all parts of the globe and have been the subject of all types of literature. Studies of mood disorders have found that people report a broad range of common symptoms. A study done by the WHO in 1983 found that most individuals diagnosed with depression reported similar symptoms such as sadness, fatigue, inability to concentrate, and sleep disturbances. People in Latino and Mediterranean countries report having headaches; Chinese and Asian cultures struggle with weakness, imbalance, and tiredness. In Middle Eastern countries, there are problems with the "heart." There are also cultural practices of underreporting psychological symptoms, and there's an Asian tendency NOT to express emotions, which can be problematic when trying to get an accurate diagnosis of depression (Goldston et al. 2008).

SCHIZOPHRENIA

About 1% of the world population suffers from **Schizophrenia**. One of the common misconceptions about this disorder is that the sufferer experiences multiple or "split" personalities, but this is not the case. Schizophrenia is a withdrawal from reality and relationships with symptoms of hallucinations and delusions and a deterioration in the everyday functioning of life. Schizophrenia is more common in men than in women in most parts of the world. Although many of the symptoms of this disorder are similar around the world, cultural, social, and economic communities influence the onset and course of schizophrenia (Phillips et al. 2004). Schizophrenia has worldwide similarities, but cross-cultural differences exist as well. Some of the similarities noted globally are lack of insight and auditory and verbal hallucinations. One difference found that surprised researchers, was that the course of the illness was more positive for those who suffer from schizophrenia and live in underdeveloped countries. Sufferers who lived in developed countries didn't do as well recovering or dealing with the illness. Collectivistic cultures had more support for members of their group suffering from mental illness such as schizophrenia because there is usually more support from extended family and the community. Those

Figure 9.3 Cultures vary in their systems of healthcare.

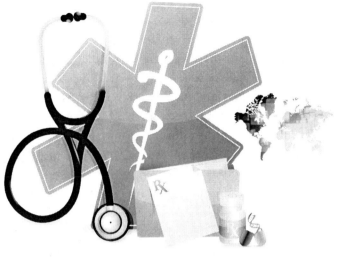

affected are usually in a married relationship and more likely to return to work full-time, which is reported to be more beneficial in recovery (Matsumoto and Juang 2013).

SUICIDE

It's hard to imagine inflicting self-harm with the intent to die when, as humans, we have such a strong will to survive. What happens in our minds that causes us to believe that we should exit this world and that life should move on without us? Surprisingly, about every 15 minutes there is a suicide in the U.S. making it the 10th leading cause of death. What's MOST surprising is that underdeveloped countries have lower suicide rates than developed countries. Nations in which people tend to be happier than people in other nations have higher suicide rates. Why would this be the case? Matsumoto suggests that people who are unhappy in an environment where most are happy could be more difficult than to reside with others who believe life is miserable and tough (Mastumoto and Juang 2013).

CULTURAL PERSPECTIVES ON SUICIDE

Suicide rates will differ worldwide depending on cultural perspectives. In America, as most of us have seen, suicide is viewed as an unnecessary tragedy and creates a much harder grieving process for family and friends. There are feelings of guilt and shame associated with suicide as those left behind struggle to know how things could have been different. In most societies suicide is taboo; however there are some differences in perspective that allow for more understanding of the act. There is group pressure NOT to commit suicide in some cultures. Religious cultures usually have lower suicide rates because they perceive the act as "self-murder" and therefore sinful. However, because of religious and ideological beliefs, suicide may be encouraged as an act of terrorism. In China, unlike most countries, suicide rates are higher for women than for men. Among some of the causes for this is the limitation on the number of children a couple may have. For many years it was limited to one child, but currently two children are allowed. While it may be hard for most Americans to understand, some Chinese parents prefer having a boy and many times girls are unwanted and uncared for which in turn leads to more suicide.

Cross-cultural research done on suicide has shown that there are three main precursors to suicide in spite of cultural background. The factors that contribute to suicide are depressive disorders, alcohol and substance abuse, and group pressure or "loss of face."

JAPAN AND SUICIDE

Most of us learned in history classes about the kamikaze pilots who willingly gave their lives by flying their planes into warships during their attack on Pearl Harbor on December 7, 1941. This was seen as an honorable act of bravery to give your life for your country. Suicide rates are still high in Japan. Suicide is seen as a reasonable way to escape failure or save yourself or loved ones from loss of face. Honor is a virtue in Japan and many perceive suicide as a type of "honorable" death. In addition, Japanese people who have suicidal thoughts are least likely to share their feelings with mental health professionals or seek help from others around them as it may be perceived as a sign of weakness or a burden to others in their collectivistic culture.

THERAPY AND HEALING OF MENTAL DISORDERS

Culture plays a crucial role in psychotherapy. **Psychotherapy** is treatment of a psychological disorder through psychological means and usually involves having verbal interactions with a licensed therapist. The idea of psychotherapy may not be understood by other cultures because for many, the symptoms are felt in the body, and *where* the illness is felt in the body differs among cultures. Americans tend to believe that we have the answers when it comes to healing mental disorders. Watch the following video clip that explains why this can be a problem.

https://www.youtube.com/watch?v=kysvXEBP-Fo

It's important to be aware of cultural differences when it comes to helping others around the world. It's an ethnocentric attitude to believe that we have the best solutions for mental healthcare. It's true that our medical doctors are trained in medicine. It's not surprising then, that they will offer medical solutions to ailments. It can't be denied that in many cases, medicinal therapy will offer the most beneficial results. There are those who believe that doctors are overprescribing and not looking for alternative care or trying to understand the underlying causes of a medical problem. This tends to be changing in America as patients realize that there are other treatment options. Turning to natural healing and natural substances to cure illness is becoming more accepted. Many are searching for solutions outside of our cultural borders.

INDIGENOUS HEALING

Indigenous healing encompasses therapeutic beliefs and practices that are rooted within a given culture. In other words, these beliefs and practices are not imported from outside cultures but are indigenously developed to treat the native population (Sue and Sue, 2007). The World Health Organization (2004) says that for most of the world, traditional healers and doctors (especially in underdeveloped countries), use native healing as a primary source of healthcare. Many of these native healers are referred to as **Shamans**. They carry with them a long history of plant-based medicines that are native to their environment as well as spiritual rituals to help heal all manner of illnesses. To understand healthcare at a global level, traditional healing must be better understood and, more importantly, integrated with Western-based health treatments as much as possible. Unlike Western bio-medical care,

Figure 9.4 Shamans who use indigenous healing practices are still common in many parts of the world.

religion and spirituality are core elements to a great number of indigenous treatments. There is no reason that the Western notion of treatment cannot be integrated on some level with indigenous therapies. We are starting to see a shift in Western practices to be more inclusive of naturally based treatments such as energy-medicine and acupuncture. As the world becomes more aware of different cultural practices due to globalization, many of these treatments found globally will continue to merge together to form new options for healthcare.

CULTURE MATCHING IN THERAPY

There are many factors that affect a therapist's diagnosis. One factor that would affect the diagnostic outcome is the cultural background of the client, as well as the therapist. The therapist may misjudge the patient's responses. In addition, the clients may express their thoughts and emotions based on their cultural norms. For example, in America, if one avoids eye contact, it can be a sign that the person lacks self-confidence, is disinterested, or has something to hide. In some cultures, it's a sign of respect to avoid eye contact when addressing a superior. This can create quite a distortion in therapy if these basic cultural behaviors are misunderstood. Another problem faced by working with someone from another culture in this setting are the biases and stereotypes one may have and not even realize it. This would definitely affect the diagnosis. Our perceptions and the way we perceive them are influenced by our knowledge of the person's cultural background.

Li-Repac (1980) investigated the effect of sociocultural differences between therapists and clients on clinical impressions, perceptions, and judgements. In her study, it was proven that a clinician's own ethnicity affected his or her perceptions of the clients. Using the same clients, Chinese therapists judged the white clients to be more severely disturbed than did the white therapists. Conversely, the white therapists viewed the Chinese clients as more depressed and inhibited than did the Chinese therapists. This study proves that cultural stereotyping can work both ways (Li-Repac 1980, p. 339).

So is it better to have a therapist and client who are from the same culture? The answer is that while there are definite benefits to a cultural match, there are some drawbacks as well. It's so nice to be understood and have the therapist know just where you're coming from. Being void of cultural biases and stereotypes is also a plus. The down side would be that through research it is shown that those therapists with the same cultural background are unable to see significant symptoms in their clients and may be underdiagnosing them (Russell et. al. 1996).

Today, at least in America, therapists are receiving additional training to become more competent in working with those who have different cultural backgrounds. Clinical trainings are incorporating culture and diversity into their programs. To prepare an effective treatment plan, a mental health professional should have more than just a basic amount of cross-cultural knowledge. The language spoken should be taken into consideration as well as the level of acculturation (how long the clients have been exposed to American culture) and an awareness of how cultural expressions represent symptoms.

Chapter 10

Cultural Identity Development and Social Interaction

Our culture, our traditions, our language are the foundations upon which we build our identity.

—Bilingualisbetter.com

Figure 10.1

Copyright © Depositphotos/iphemant.

Erik Erikson and Abraham Maslow both agree that one of the major developmental tasks for every person is to establish a personal identity. Our self-concept is based on our cultural environment. I don't think anyone can separate his or her culture from whom he or she has become.

153

SELF-AWARENESS AND PERSONAL IDENTITY

The following paragraphs explain in more detail how we develop our sense of identity.

Reading 10.1

THE GRADUAL PROCESS OF SELF-AWARENESS

Self-awareness begins early in life. By about nine months of age the average child starts to differentiate the self from others (Harter, 1983). At the age of 18 months the typical child will have a developed a sense of self-awareness and can react with more emotion to pictures of themselves than to unrelated people. Gradually as our self-knowledge grows, the self takes on other attributes. If lucky our cultural environment nurture positive self-attributes leading to feelings of competence or self-efficacy. Individuals living in less stimulating cultures are not as fortunate as some societies place limits on what is possible centered in the self-concept that affects individual plans for work and development.

A biological basis for self-awareness is suggested by research in other species that demonstrates self-awareness (Gallup, 1977, 1997). In one study the experimenter initially placed a mirror in the cage of chimpanzees until it became a familiar object. Afterwards the experimenter placed an odorless red dye on the animals' ear or brow. The animals recognized that something had changed and responded with immediately touching the dyed area. Studies with dolphins and other animals demonstrate a similar pattern of self-recognition (Mitchell, 2003).

KNOWING ABOUT THE SELF

Using similar techniques with toddlers, researchers found that self-recognition is present at around age two (Lewis, 1997; Povinelli, Landau, & Perilloux, 1996). Over time the child begins to incorporate psychological attributes including more complex feelings and thoughts. This social self is based on how we are evaluated by others (Hart & Damon, 1986). As we develop more complex beliefs and feelings about the social self, we also begin to project ourselves to some degree into the future. From these initial experiences with the family, educational system, and the broader culture the social self gradually emerges.

The self-concept is the knowledge we have of ourselves, that we exist separately from others, and have our own unique properties. As part of our self-knowledge we develop a belief system that governs behavior. Do we live in a world of chaos or order? Do we believe we can accomplish important goals? Can other people be trusted? This complex web of beliefs in turn contributes to whether we approach or avoid others, impact our feelings of self-esteem, and provides a concept of what we can become in the future called a possible self. In the process of maturation children gradually place less emphasis on concrete physical descriptions of the self, as more awareness is centered on complex psychological states including thoughts, feelings, and the evaluations of others (Harter, 2003; Hart & Damon, 1986).

THE MEANING OF SELF-ESTEEM

Culture is an important dimension affecting self-esteem. In independent ego-based cultures self-esteem is connected to personal accomplishments. On the other hand, in interdependent cultures self-esteem is based more on the connectedness to others and relationships. Therefore social approval is a more significant component of overall self-esteem in the collectivistic societies. In individualistic cultures while self-esteem derive from individual accomplishments and achievement, it does not follow that accomplishments are unimportant in interdependent cultures, or that relationships are not significant in independent cultures, but rather that the cultural values are the mediators of these common factors in the self and in self-esteem. Social approval is probably of significance in all societies as it is directly related to survival and inclusion. However, self-worth reflects at least in part how the individual conform to central cultural values.

An important contribution to the self-concept is our self-evaluations or self-esteem. Self-esteem is evaluative based judgments of personal morality and whether in our own eyes we are satisfied or dissatisfied with our performance and behavior. Global self-esteem can be measured by surveys and is related to our need for approval (e.g. Larsen, 1969). The lower our self-esteem the more we have a need for affirmation and approval by others and society. High self-esteem, on the other hand, is associated with setting appropriate goals, using feedback from others to progress, and enjoying positive experiences to the fullest extent possible (Wood, Heimpel, & Michela, 2003). When experiencing rejection or frustration, those with high self-esteem will find a silver lining. High self-esteem people are adaptable and are persistent in working toward goal and have the ability when frustrated to envision alternative goals (Sommer & Baumeister, 2002). High self-esteem people will look at the past through rose-colored glasses and this selective positive memory bias may in turn support their higher self-esteem (Christensen, Wood, & Barrett, 2003).

On the other hand, people with low self-esteem not only think poorly of themselves, but the negative self-conceptions have other unfortunate consequences. Low self-esteem persons are more pessimistic about the future, tend to obsess about their negative moods, are more concerned about the opinions of others, and have higher needs for approval (Heimpel, Wood, Marshall, & Brown, 2002). Low self-esteem is also reflected in negative estimations of competence or self-efficacy and in self-loathing. On the other hand, those with positive feelings toward the self not only like themselves, but have feelings of competence (Tafarodi, Marshall, & Milne, 2003). As we shall see throughout this chapter and what follows, the cultural context matters. Members of Asian cultures, for example, are less self-enhancing in explicit ways, but enhance more in implicit ways (Koole, Dijksterhuis, & Van Knippenberg, 2001).

CULTURE AS A SOURCE OF THE SELF-CONCEPT

In chapter 1 we introduced the concept of individualistic and collectivistic cultures. It is now time to apply this cultural division to the formation of the social self. We shall see that these cultural differences created independent and interdependent selves that have applications throughout this chapter. Culture has profound effects in socialization and produces predictable differences in self-concepts. Western societies found in North America and Europe has inculcated social values significant to successful adaptation and survival in the capitalist model. The term "rugged individualism" points to a person who is first and foremost independent and was able to cope with the hazards of life in early United States. In that cultural environment each man was a king in his own house, and society was preoccupied then as now with individual self-actualization.

In Asian societies, on the other hand, we have ancient cultures that had to adapt to high levels of physical density of their large populations. Physical density is not experienced as crowding in Asia to the same degree it would be experienced in the West, because the highly developed structures of courtesy evolved to meet the need for personal space and privacy. Hall (1976) thought of independent societies, as "low-context cultures" where social roles while not unimportant mattered less. Therefore a person from independent cultures would more or less act the same regardless of the changing context of behavior or the situation. *In interdependent cultures on the other hand, the social context matters a great deal, and the individual's behavior will change dependent on the specific role played by the participant.* In interdependent cultures the behavior of the self would differ depending on role expectation and the person would behave in ways that are appropriate in interactions with parents, peers, or colleagues. As we shall see, in Western societies the bias toward independence leads to attribution errors where we underestimate the influence of the situation and attribute behavior primarily to individual traits.

In recent years social psychologists have carried out many cross-cultural studies on how motivations, emotions, and behaviors are shaped by cultural conceptions of the self (Markus & Kitayama, 1991a; Rhee, Uleman, Lee, & Roman, 1995; Triandis, 1995). From this accumulated research the cultures characterized as promoting values of self-independence are found primarily in the West. In Western societies the self is seen as autonomous, distinct and separate from other members of society. Consequently explanations for behavior are sought within the individual's personality. Not only is independence a fundamental value, but Westerners also believe that the main object of socialization is to create independent children (Kitayama, 1992). The self is therefore described as composed of individual attributes (Trafimov, Triandis, & Goto, 1991). Achievements are seen as primarily the result of individual and distinctive efforts and where family or society played at best peripheral roles.

In the interdependent cultures of Asia and in countries of the developing world the self is perceived as part of the larger social context. The self is not construed apart from other people, but rather as connected to family and larger social organizations. The willingness of people to go on suicide missions like the kamikaze pilots of Japan is related to the interdependent self-construal where country and emperor are part of the self. Western combatants may also fight with great courage, however, self-sacrifice is best elicited when there is some possibility if not probability of survival. In interdependent societies the self is completely embedded in the roles and duties of social relationships. Culture therefore determines to a large extent self-knowledge and self-esteem, as well as self-presentations and impression management. The self is connected to the attributes of others, is not seen as distinctive, but associated with family and society (Bochner, 1994). These cultural differences are thought to profoundly affect how individuals think about themselves, how they relate to others in society, and in what motivates their behavior (Markus & Kitayama, 1994b).

Studies have shown that Americans achieve primarily for personal reasons, whereas those from interdependent societies strive to achieve group goals (Lyengar & Lepper, 1999). It is the personal nature of tasks and objectives that motivates behavior in the West, whereas Asian students are motivated more by group goals. Consequently students in the West are more likely to select careers or tasks in which they have experienced previous success and which had been rewarding in the past. The career choices of Asians, on the other hand, are not based on such personal expectations or prior performance (Oishi & Diener, 2003).

These cultural differences in self-construal also affect how we organize information in memory (Woike, Gershkovich, Piorkowski, & Polo, 1999). *People in independent cultures disregard the social context in memory formation, and think of events in personal terms.* Elections in the United States are typically about the personal attributes of candidates where the social context or genuine political proposals matters little. Typically this personalized political process manipulates the indifferent electorate to disregard political programs in the search for the "right" person.

There are some researchers who feel these cultural differences in self-construal make intercultural communication very difficult (Kitayama & Markus, 1994b). Yet, at the end of the day we must remember that these cultural differences are abstractions and there are always more differences found within than between social groups. In independent cultures there are many people with interdependent self-construal, particularly among women (Cross, Bacon, & Morris, 2000; Cross & Vick, 2001). In interdependent societies, on the other hand, there are also people whose self-construal is independent. Further, migration and globalization is changing the world. For example, within [the] United States and Europe there are many immigrants who come from cultures with interdependent self-construal. Many migrants work hard in Western societies not for individual benefit, but so they can send most of their earnings back to the home country. Globalization is also producing more converging values for example, an increasing emphasis on human rights in nearly all societies, and as that takes its course in the future we must reevaluate the cultural differences discussed above.

It could be argued that the topic of human development should be a discussion for Chapter 3: Enculturation and Socialization. However, as we are discussing identity and self-esteem, it seemed fitting to include Brofenbrenner's ecological systems theory of human development with identity development.

In Brofenbrenner's view, human development is a dynamic interactive process between individuals and various ecologies that range from the proximal, immediate environment to

Figure 10.2 Brofenbrenner's ecological systems theory of human development.

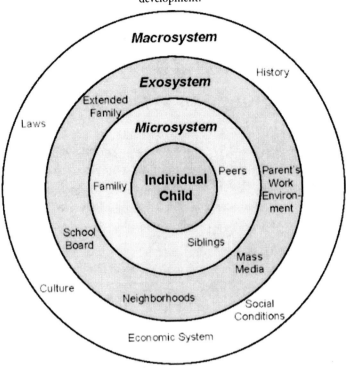

the more distal (Mastumoto and Juang 2013). As you can see in the diagram in image 10.2, there are different environments in one's upbringing that include the *microsystem*, the immediate surroundings such as the family school and peer group with which children directly interact; the *mesosystem*, the linkage between microsystems such as between school and family; the *exosystem*, the context that indirectly affects children such as a parent's workplace; and the *macrosystem* that includes culture, religion, and society. There's also another factor to this system which is called the *chronosystem*, the influence of time and history on the other systems. Broffenbrenner posits that the only way to understand how a child develops is to consider the child in *relation* to his or her cultural environment. In addition, he explains that a child is not a passive participant in this process. Children do not simply absorb cultural information but can contribute to their own personal development by interacting with people and groups around them. A child's identity is certainly influenced by culture, as we can see from Brofenbrenner's work, however, it's important to keep in mind that each child brings his or her own disposition and personality to these interactions.

PERSONALITY TRAITS

THE FIVE FACTOR MODEL OF PERSONALITY

The FFM or the Five Factor Model of Personality is a concept that was built on decades of cross-cultural research and has helped many to understand the relationship between personality and culture. There appear to be five basic personality dimensions that are found all over the world. You can see these dimensions in image 10.3. They are *neuroticism, extraversion, openness to experience, agreeableness*, and *conscientiousness*. There have been numerous studies

Figure 10.3 There are basic personality traits that can be found in every culture.

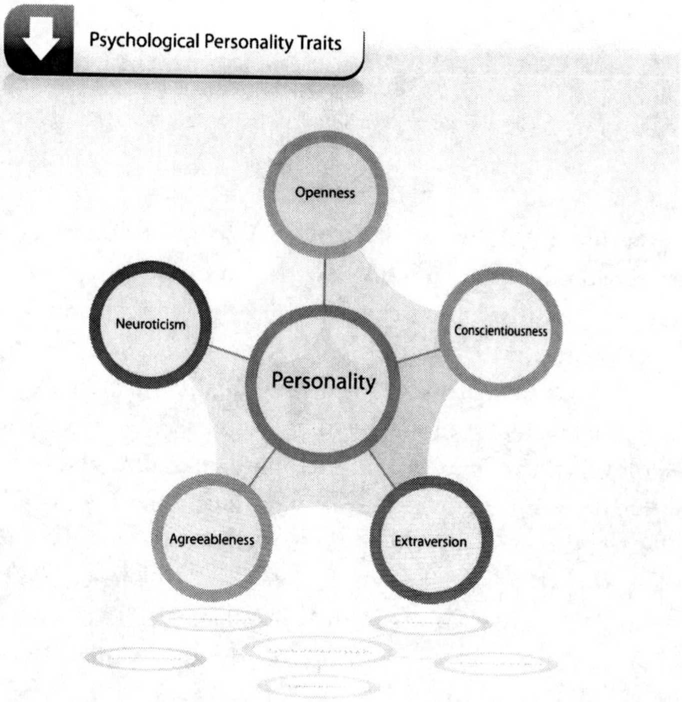

Copyright © Depositphotos/cteconsulting.

done to test this theory, yet it continues to seem a valid assessment of universal characteristics. Each study conducted included more cultures and different types of personality testing, including NEO personality inventory. The newly revised version of this test includes 240 items where respondents rate the degree to which they agree or disagree that the item is characteristic of them. Some researchers debate whether there may be even more common traits around the world, but according to the work that has been done, the Five Factor Model still stands as an accurate assessment of universal personality traits.

OTHER TRAITS ASSOCIATED WITH THE "BIG FIVE"

There are an additional 30 traits that fall under these five major traits. **Neuroticism** includes traits such as anxiety, angry hostility, depression, self-consciousness, impulsiveness, and vulnerability. **Extraversion** includes warmth, gregariousness, assertiveness, activity, excitement seeking, and positive emotions. **Openness** involves the traits of fantasy, aesthetics, feelings, actions, ideas, and values. Included with **Agreeableness** is trust, straightforwardness, altruism, compliance, modesty, and tender-mindedness. Finally, **Conscientiousness** includes competence, order, dutifulness, achievement striving, self-discipline, and deliberation. It's important to note that there may be different names used to describe these same traits depending on the researcher, but these are the basic descriptions of personality characteristics worldwide.

CULTURAL INFLUENCE ON PERSONALITY DEVELOPMENT

Cross-cultural research is interested in finding similarities as well as differences in personality traits worldwide. Culture-specific personality traits have been found during these studies and are referred to as **indigenous personalities.** These personality traits tend to be found only within a specific culture. These findings on indigenous personalities have led to another concept known as cultural perspective and includes work done by Shweder, Markus, and Kitayama (1998). Read the following paragraph that explains the cultural perspective to personality.

The cultural perspective assumes that psychological processes, in this case the nature of functioning of personality, are not just influenced by culture but are thoroughly culturally constituted. In turn, the cultural perspective assumes that personalities behaving in concert create the culture. Culture and personality are most productively analyzed together as a dynamic of mutual constitution.... one cannot be reduced to the other ... A cultural psychological approach does not automatically assume that all behavior can be explained with the same set of categories and dimensions and first asks whether a given dimension, concept, or category is meaningful and how it is used in a given cultural context (Markus and Kitayama 1998, p. 66).

It's nice to know as we do cross-cultural research, that we can find fascinating differences between cultures, yet there are also ties that bind us together that make us human. Common personality traits (i.e., the Five Factor Model of Personality) is yet another way that we can link together as humans. Each culture tends to have an *indigenous personality* as well, that is directly connected to the particular culture, and according to the excerpt above, one cannot survive without the other. People living in all different parts of the world, yet sharing common traits, can bring us closer together as we continue to study and learn about each other.

Figure 10.4 Minority students have unique challenges as they struggle to find out who they are and where they belong.

Copyright © Depositphotos/rmarmion.

When we are living in our own culture surrounded by those who understand us the most, it can instill confidence and help us to understand who we are. Living where there is a significant amount of cultural diversity can be an overwhelming challenge for many. Suddenly we are in unfamiliar territory and may begin to question who we are and how we fit in. This can be especially hard for teens. Watch the following video clip about ethnic identity as a teenager.

https://www.youtube.com/watch?v=MfisBVoreS8

The following video offers an interesting perspective on leaving home to actually *find* who you really are and to appreciate your own culture in a new and different way.

https://www.youtube.com/watch?v=fTt8jdK1lGI

CULTURAL VALUES AND DIMENSIONS

Hofstede (2001) researched 72 different countries and 117,000 multinational employees to come up with five work-related values from different societies (see image 10.5). These

Figure 10.5

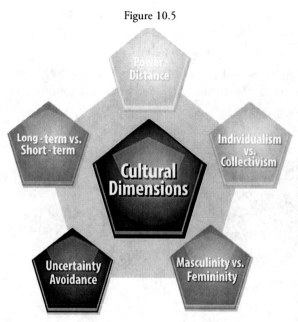

Copyright © Depositphotos/kgtohbu.

research findings on cultural values have been very important to the study of cross-cultural psychology.

One of the most important aspects to the value dimensions is **Individualism vs. Collectivism**, which is discussed in more detail in Chapter 1. The behaviors and perspectives of one working in a group who is from a collectivistic culture could vary greatly from those thoughts and perspectives of one raised in an individualistic culture. Another cultural dimension is **Power Distance** which refers to a hierarchical social relationship. There is more conformity and obedience to authority in cultures that have a high power distance. **Uncertainty Avoidance** is a cultural value dimension and is the degree to which people feel threatened by the unknown or circumstances in which there is uncertainty. Cultures will vary with the level of discomfort with uncertainty. In cultures that have a high level of uncertainty, emotional expression will be at a minimum. **Masculinity vs. Femininity** is a fourth dimension from Hofstede's research. Men, in many cultures, are more dominant and assertive than women. Although sex roles have been changing over the last few decades, it is still a source of controversy and conflict in many cultures around the world. This dimension of masculinity and femininity is the extent to which a culture will emphasize the traditional gender roles at home and at work. Hofstede and Bond (1984) added a fifth dimension called **Long-Term vs. Short-Term Outlook**. This value includes the willingness a culture has to delay gratification. Many cultures expect immediate satisfaction while others are patient and focus more on long-term relationships and delay gratification in several ways, including material objects as well as emotional needs. In the work place, these cultural values should be considered as they can greatly affect the efficiency and productivity of a group working together.

CULTURAL VALUE DIMENSIONS AND THE IMPACT ON THE WORKPLACE

One's cultural background greatly affects the way he or she will perform certain tasks in the work place. This is a topic that is still being studied. Should a prospective employee's cultural background match the organization for less conflict and more production? The cultural values one acquires through the process of enculturation could make a great impact on a company either negatively or positively. Studies have shown that employees who had values that were congruent with those of their supervisor were more satisfied and committed to their job. On the other hand, some evidence exists that the employee/company fit may not be that important (Nyambegera, Daniels, and Sparrow 2001). Furthermore, who's to say what constitutes a successful match? Perhaps some "mismatches" may surprisingly be more beneficial for an organization. At least one study has shown that with the right balance of collectivism and individualism, innovation and entrepreneurship is at its highest, and highly individualistic or highly collectivistic corporations are at the lowest (Morris, Avila, and Allen 1993).

Some of the differences that are found in organizations due to cultural values are as follows. Employees who have a low power distance are less afraid of disagreeing with supervisors and show more cooperation in working with others; those with a high power distance will fear disagreeing with the boss and are less likely to trust each other; those who have a low uncertainty avoidance value don't mind some competition between employees and may consider breaking rules for what they see as a good reason, and they understand that conflicts can be normal when working with others; and those who are high in uncertainty avoidance will not agree with competition between employees, don't believe company rules should be broken under any circumstances, and don't want to see any conflict in the workplace.

Other differences in those from collectivistic and individualistic cultures are listed in more detail here: those organizations that foster high masculinity will have fewer women in jobs where there are men, and there are greater value differences between men and women in the same jobs, and organizations with higher femininity will see more women in jobs where there are men and smaller value differences between men and women in the same jobs. How these cultural dimensions manifest themselves in the workplace is explained further in the paragraph below.

Hofstede's dimensions are useful in understanding cultural differences in attitudes about work. For instance, people in Low Power Distance cultures have a stronger perceived work ethic and a strong disbelief that people dislike work whereas the opposite is true for people in High Power Distance cultures. Duty in life appeals to people in collectivistic cultures while enjoyment in life appeals to people in individualistic cultures. People in higher performance capabilities in Masculine cultures feel empowered to make decisions and seek opportunities to voice their opinions whereas people with less capabilities in Feminine cultures value the importance of nurturing people with lower capability (van den Bos et al. 2013).

Tolerance, inter-cultural dialogue and respect for diversity are more essential than ever in a world where peoples are becoming more and more closely interconnected.

—Kofi Annan, Former Secretary-General of the United Nations

THE IMPORTANCE OF CONTEXT IN SOCIAL BEHAVIOR

Cultures vary on the extent that people pay attention to context. Context includes the level of voice, eye contact, posture, and orientation of the body, as well as the distance between bodies. Triandis explains that even the extent to which one person is touching another and where he or she is touching the body can convey meaning (Lonner and Malpass 1994). It can be very difficult to change our behaviors when interacting with someone from another culture even if we understand the differences. Being aware of these differences however, may allow us to consciously come part way to bridge the gap. Japan is a culture that has a very high context society. Cultures high in context, according to Triandis, are societies where people have to maintain long-term relationships and are relatively simple. There are less direct and more subtle interactions in cultures where context is important. There's a great need to "save face" or not make another person uncomfortable by saying "no" directly. There are indirect ways to say the same thing through signs or gestures. The United States, as well as other European cultures like Germany or the Netherlands, are relatively low context cultures. Still, members of these cultures will pay attention to nonverbal cues, but it is on a much smaller scale. The United States has a higher context than Switzerland, however. In Switzerland, things are explained very clearly and sometimes may be misunderstood as rude or blunt.

Figure 10.6 Working and communicating with a multi-cultural group in the workplace can be successful when basic differences in cultural perspectives are understood and respected.

COLLECTIVISM VS. INDIVIDUALISM AND THE INFLUENCE ON SOCIAL BEHAVIOR

Harry C. Triandis is a professor of psychology and has helped establish cross-cultural psychology as a separate, scientific discipline. Referring to culture and social behavior, Triandis explains that "The contrast between Collectivism and Individualism is one of the most important cultural differences in social behavior" (Triandis 2001).

In the following paragraphs, Triandis compares and contrasts individualistic and collectivistic behaviors in different aspects of daily life.

Attitudes—Collectivists value interdependence. They believe children should live with their parents before marriage and that their own parents will live with them until they die. Individualists want independence. While close family and friends are important in these decisions, ultimately, they choose the best individual path.

Goals—in a collectivistic culture, one will choose the goals of the in-group even if it is in conflict with personal goals. The individualist will choose his or her own personal goals.

Values—some of the values that are stressed by collectivists are security, obedience, duty, in-group harmony, hierarchy, and personalized relationships. The values stressed by individualists are pleasure, winning the competition, achievement, freedom, autonomy, and fair exchange.

Social behavior—collectivistic cultures know their in-group very well and interact with them often. They know very little about people outside of this group. Individualists know a wide range of people but may not be close to any of them (Lonner and Malpass 1994).

The meaning of work is different based on collectivism and individualism, as well. Read the following excerpt about attitudes and work.

In American culture, it is easy to think of work simply as a means to make a living. In other cultures (especially collectivistic), work may be seen more as fulfilling an obligation to a larger group. In this situation, we would expect to find less movement of individuals from one job to another because of the individual's social obligations toward the work organization to which he or she belongs and to the people comprising that organization. In individualistic cultures, it is easier to consider leaving one job and going to another because it is easier to separate jobs from the self. A different job will just as easily accomplish the same goals (Mastumoto and Juang 2013).

It is clear that being raised in a collectivistic or individualistic culture affects not only our own personal identity but also the way we view the world and those around us. One of the biggest problems most of us will face is working with others and not taking into account one's cultural values or worldviews. A little bit of research and understanding of other cultural perspectives could prevent frustration and unfair analysis of behaviors.

Chapter 11

Acculturation

It is not the strongest or the most intelligent who will survive but those who can best manage change.

—Charles Darwin

Figure 11.1

Reading 11.1

We immigrants never feel like we have a home. I always miss home and have idealistic and romantic views of it and cannot wait to go home especially when people keep asking me when I would go back for good. It is like "Hello, this is home!" I eventually decided maybe this is not home, then when I go back home I feel so awkward because I notice too quickly how my people have no boundaries. They will visit you without any announcement and stay forever. They tell me how "Americanized" I have become and even say I have an American accent and American values. Then I feel restless and miss [my U.S.] home. Sometimes I have to bribe my way out of everything. I remember I once planned to meet some friends at the park at 2 pm. I was at the park exactly at 2 pm and they showed up at 5 pm when I was leaving. I was so angry that they were late and they laughed at me for a long time and called me an "Uptight American Lady." They laughed at how quickly I have forgotten the African "time." They laughed so hard I wanted to take the next plane back to the U.S. I said to myself, I can't believe how they did not respect me! But that was not the issue. They did not mean to disrespect me. I just have to remember that it is a different culture. I have to remember to switch my roles quickly. Recently I was mulling over this and was wondering where do I really fit? I realized I honestly do not fit anywhere. Americans quickly notice I have an accent and ask me when I am going back to where I came from and Ghanaians can tell that I have acquired some American tastes and values. I must say it is very difficult for me to relax at either place. The only place I can truly call my home is when I sit alone with myself and my thoughts, in my room all alone.

—Adjoa, 40+-Year-Old Ghanaian Immigrant Woman

This experience of the woman from Ghana in the story from *Multicultural Psychology* (Mio, Barker, and Rodriguez 2016), illustrates how hard it is to live outside of your own culture. Furthermore, after spending some time in another culture, it may be hard to return and readjust to your native culture. There are myriad hardships and struggles that a person must face when he or she moves to a new culture, especially if it differs greatly from his or her own. We must become more aware of the acculturation process that immigrants and refugees experience. **Acculturation** is the process of individual change and adaptation as a

Jeffrey Mio, Lori Barker, and Melanie M. Domenech Rodriguez, from "Immigrants, Refugees, and the Acculturation Process," *Multicultural Psychology, 4th ed.*, pp. 145. Copyright © 2016 by Oxford University Press. Reprinted with permission.

result of continuous contact with a new, distinct culture. Newcomers to this country who are unable to adjust to their new surroundings often experience **acculturative stress** (also known as "culture shock") which is a distressful, psychological reaction to an unfamiliar environment. People who come from other countries are faced with language barriers that can be very difficult to overcome (Mio, Barker, and Rodriquez 2016). In addition to the challenge of learning a new language and being unable to communicate with those around you, there are often differences in family structures, body language, emotional displays, education, and most certainly, dietary changes. All of these can have a negative effect on anyone encountering a new culture.

Figure 11.2 Both immigrants and refugees can struggle to find meaning in a new environment and lifestyle. Many encounter confusion as well as risk.

Copyright © Depositphotos/lightsource.

IMMIGRANTS AND REFUGEES

Many use the terms immigrant and refugee interchangeably, however, there are distinct differences between them. Immigrants and refugees may have very different experiences when resettling in a new culture, but there are some common experiences they share.

IMMIGRANTS

Immigrants are those who have a choice to come to a new country. They may leave for job opportunities or better living conditions. They usually have the choice to go home if they decide they don't like the change. Immigrants may also have some help in finding a job (Cheal 2001). Immigrants usually have social support from those in their new country and in the country they left behind. Immigrants plan their exit, look for a new place to live, have a chance to say goodbye to family and friends, and even learn a bit about their new cultural norms and customs. They may have a chance to learn a few words in the new language as well. There also may be support networks in the new country that are aware of their arrival and welcome them to their new life (Cheal 2001). It's not uncommon for an immigrant to spend a significant amount of time between the host and native countries (Bolzman, Fibbi, and Vial 2006). As we have learned from the story of the woman from Ghana, this situation

Figure 11.3 Refugees have the added burden of not knowing where they will go. They are taken wherever they can find a safe place to start a new life.

Copyright © Depositphotos/Xarlyxa.

has its own unique challenges as many find that they don't quite fit into either culture and no longer know which culture to call home.

REFUGEES

Refugees differ in many ways from immigrants. **Refugees** have been forced to flee their homeland because of a threat to their life, safety, or for fear of persecution. Many will escape with nothing more than the clothes on their back. Most refugees do not choose where they will go but are assigned to whatever country that can offer them a safe place to live their lives. Because of the violence that they have fled, many refugees have the added burden of not knowing if their families have survived. Not only are they unable to have a continuing relationship with their family, but they must also suffer the trauma of wondering if they are alive. Most refugees will be unable to return to their homeland to visit due to political unrest and many times, excessive damage, and therefore, no home or community in which to return. Unlike immigrants, refugees don't have a chance to prepare and say goodbye to loved ones, and they know very little, if anything at all, about the country that will be their new home. Refugees do well when they have support from others who speak their language and especially those from their native country. One of the negative aspects however, is relying too heavily on your support system and not venturing outside of the group to learn the new language or local customs.

Please watch the following documentary on refugees who have been resettled in America.

http://www.pbs.org/video/2262091142/

This documentary offers great insight into the plight of refugees in America. Most viewing this video are surprised at how little time there is before benefits run out, leaving the refugees to find their own way. Not surprisingly, there are some extended mental health issues for many refugees.

Frequently, refugees experience deaths in their families, threats of violence or death, separation from important family members, and other forms of trauma. Trauma and adaptation intersect in complex ways. Refugees exposed to trauma and loss can experience symptoms of posttraumatic stress disorder (PTSD) and prolonged grief disorder (PGD), which vary according to adaptation to the new culture (Mio et. al. 2016).

There are many ways that members of the host country may help. Offering clothing, furniture, and food are welcomed and needed. It's important to note however, that anyone can help by simply being kind and understanding, offering a smile, sharing community resources, and giving a little personal time. Learning about the lives of refugees and asking them questions about their native country is not only a great way to learn about new cultures, but offers them the opportunity to share with others what they know and love, which could be a therapeutic benefit in the adjustment to their new world.

WHAT DOES THIS MEAN TO ME?

Have you ever misjudged someone from another culture? Were you previously aware of some of the challenges he or she must face? Have you been a part of any organization that has helped immigrants and refugees adapt to their new culture? Do you take the time to say hello and ask questions to those you know are from another culture? How can doing these things help us as well as help these new residents?

COMMON CHALLENGES FOR IMMIGRANTS AND REFUGEES

LANGUAGE BARRIER

Not only is it a tremendous challenge to learn the words of a new language but the *manner* of communication can vary significantly between cultures. The distance between bodies, facial expressions, body language, intonation, and directness vs. indirectness can all have a great impact on the acculturation process and acquisition of language. Many newcomers may feel that Americans are too direct and seem rude. You can probably guess that the older immigrants generally have a harder time adjusting since their ways of life are more engrained, and it may be harder for them to learn the new rules of a culture.

Those who learn the language quickly within a group usually have more opportunities than those who do not. It's much easier for young immigrants to practice speaking the language because they simply have more exposure to others from the host country throughout the day. Older generations may feel useless and insecure as the younger generations learn the language and customs, then translate and teach their parents and grandparents. Family dynamics are disrupted and, in turn, can cause emotional upheaval within new immigrant groups, as well. The respected and valued parents and grandparents from a previous postfigurative culture become the students and are learning from the younger generation, which may be a huge change from previous relationships. In the paragraphs below, the process of acculturation is explained in more detail by Mio, Barker, and Rodriguez (2016).

Reading 11.2

EMPLOYMENT

My wife and I thought how wonderful it will be to move from a third-world country to the United States. I had a degree as a chemical engineer and my wife was willing to stay home and care for our three young children. Most of our family lived here in the U.S. and have told many stories of how much easier it was to get jobs. One thing I didn't consider was how my degree was "no good" because I earned it from elsewhere other than the U.S. They said I need re-certification, which was a nicer way of saying that I needed to go back to school and learn "their way." Well, I couldn't do that because we had no money, and we had three children. My wife was unemployed and the rest of our family had to work to maintain their own household. I work at an ARCO gas station now and we've gotten robbed twice. I want to feel hopeful, but it has gotten harder and harder. I guess I just have to be thankful that I have a job. I want to go back "home," but we feel like it will be harder since most of our family is here.

—Andy, 30+-Year-Old Asian Immigrant Man

According to Hong and Ham (2001), immigrants often cite greater freedom, a more stable political environment, and better opportunity for their children as reasons for immigration. Once they are settled in the United States, however, prolonged low-income employment or underemployment can eventually take its toll. Lacking English-language skills and enjoying only limited social support, most immigrants and refugees are forced to find employment in ethnic communities that are also limited in growth and income. Immigrants who have sufficient financial resources attempt to establish local businesses but must do so in high-crime neighborhoods. Some groups, such as Korean Americans (Hong & Ham, 2001), have financial assets tied up in their small businesses, which prevents them from moving into more favorable businesses or neighborhoods. Other groups settle into factory jobs and other low-paying, intensive manual labor that requires many hours.

Not only do these individuals face limited employment opportunities, but once they do find employment, their premigration experiences, limited English, and physical characteristics also become reasons for employers to discriminate against them. Promotions are nearly impossible, even for those who have held prestigious positions in their countries of origin. Degrees held by immigrants before their move are not as marketable in the United States, and they are forced to accept jobs with much lower status. Decline in status lowers self-esteem and increases disillusionment, and these factors can eventually cause family distress. For some individuals who have some social or familial support, further education to obtain equivalent credentials is possible.

For others, the necessity of making ends meet makes such opportunities impossible. Most migrating people recognize that they need to attend English classes to move forward with employment, but they cannot always do so. According to Gans (2009), although both immigrants and refugees suffer downward mobility due to limitations in employment opportunities, immigrants may suffer a bit more due to the significant differences between their employment in their country and their lack of ability in attaining similar status in the United States. For refugees, migration to another country involves issues dealing more with their survival and personal freedom as opposed to simply trying to pursue a better life. They most likely have lost their jobs and social status before leaving their host country (Gans, 2009).

Individuals who are unable to master the English language are easily taken advantage of and discriminated against by employers and other employees. These individuals may be forced to accept conditions that do not meet minimal legal standards, but their lack of education and their need to feed their families force them to tolerate such treatment and working conditions. Some immigrants who are able to establish businesses are leery of taking their small businesses outside the ethnic communities because they know that thriving within a bigger cosmopolitan setting is nearly impossible. Although some do dream that their established businesses within smaller, ethnic communities are only a stepping-stone to a well-accepted and profitable venture, such dreams rarely become a reality. To clinicians and other lay people, these people present a picture of resilience, determination, content, and noble self-sacrifice (Hong & Ham, 2001). Yet underneath such external appearances can lie severe stress, doubt, and frustration (Hong, 1989; Hong & Ham, 2001).

EDUCATION

Some immigrants in the United States have had some secondary and more advanced education in their countries of origin. However, other immigrants and most refugees have limited education, which can be a major problem when they attempt to find employment that pays well. Some adult immigrants who are able to go back to school, raise a family, and work at the same time can face problems of overstress, family discord, and marital conflict. Therefore, older immigrants and refugees often place the hope for higher education on their children.

Unfortunately for immigrant children, education can also cause stress within the individual and the family system. Immigrant children who attended school in their countries of origin have a difficult time adjusting to the U.S. school system. For most immigrant children, the values within the school system in the United States differ greatly from the values in their own countries. In many places, such as Mexico and Asian countries, respect for educators is demanded just as much as respect for parents. Talking back and holding an opinion that conflicts with a teacher's opinion are not tolerated in some countries.

Parents begin to have conflicts with children who rebel against the old ways. Change that is adaptive within the classroom is often brought into the home, which reinforces parents' thinking about the U.S. educational culture. Some parents become so worried about how their children will turn out after finishing their education that they choose to take the children out of school and place them in the job market. Laws mandating that minors attend school are ignored, and tension increases among the school system, the parents, and the children. Parents who hold traditional values are often viewed as rigid by their children or those in the host culture. This perception can lead these children or authorities in the host culture to discount the parents' beliefs, even though some of these beliefs may be legitimate.

Although we highlight the preceding issues as major considerations in attempting to comprehend the experiences of immigrants and refugees, they are only some of the many issues that relate to the process of acculturation. How individuals adapt to the

Figure 11.4 Children who are relocated to America are given an opportunity to go to school and are given extra time for learning the language and culture.

Copyright © Depositphotos/rmarmion.

differences between their country of origin and their host country may determine their success. In defining the success of immigrants and refugees, we should not look at the success of individuals who have lived in the United States all their lives.

Some migrating individuals equate success with fulfilling basic needs such as food and shelter. Long-time citizens of this country also face unemployment and obstacles in attempting to achieve the American dream while we keep our gates open to others. However, individual-level arguments regarding the suitability of immigration policies ignore larger social and political forces that create the incentives for immigration such as job opportunities (Camarota & Jensenius, 2009) for both low-income earners but also for professionals that are in low supply and high demand in the United States. Furthermore, negative attitudes toward immigration ignore important gains made by society at large, often at the cost of immigrants. For example, the Social Security Administration estimates a $12 billion infusion into Social Security, offering a substantial protection to the program (Goss et al., 2013).

At an individual level, it is important to also consider that if some people have the greater advantages of family and social support, knowledge of the language, and educational and occupational opportunities, and still struggle to succeed within this culture, imagine how difficult it must be to pursue the American dream for those who are not as privileged and who lack basic language skills and cultural knowledge.

Because an individual's level of acculturation can determine his or her success, we will take a more elaborate look at what is involved in the acculturation process. In the next section, we apply the process of acculturation to "natural citizens" as well as to immigrants and refugees.

ETHNIC MINORITY POPULATIONS

Several researchers have developed "models of acculturation" for minorities in a host country. The perspectives for American ethnic minority groups are explained in the paragraphs below.

Reading 11.3

California to some, can be very confusing. I always thought of California as a melting pot of a bunch of different races and cultures. It is because of this that people start developing their own culture and identity by living in California. I think I'm at that point of understanding where I stand with my peers and with myself being Korean American. I have visited Korea a few times and whenever I'm there, people are able to point out that I'm from America. Just the way I speak Korean or the way I dress. If I'm in America, people say I'm Korean, but people in Korea, say that I'm American. This makes me a bit confused sometimes. It's hard to say who I am because even at the age of 23, I'm still trying to figure out my place in the world and with myself. At this point I would give myself the title as Korean American just because my blood is Korean but my attitude is American. Being a person from two different cultures sometimes gives me more to appreciate. For now I think I'm comfortable with that.

—Kenny, 20+-Year-Old Korean American Man

ACCULTURATION OF ETHNIC MINORITY POPULATIONS

LaFramboise proposed a model of acculturation from her American Indian perspective that was designed to describe the acculturation process of American ethnic minority populations (LaFramboise, Coleman, & Gerton, 1993). Similar to the Berry model, the LaFramboise model (Table 11.1) includes *assimilationists*, who are also defined as those who completely absorb the dominant culture. Although assimilationists believe that complete absorption into the dominant culture ensures acceptance, they may experience rejection from the members of their own cultural group. Assimilationists also lose their original cultural identity, which may later cause guilt and isolation.

Acculturated—competent in host culture but maintains own cultural identity as more essential.

LaFramboise and associates define individuals who are competent in a second culture without completely accepting it as being **acculturated**. This group seems to mirror integrationists in that people are able to show competence within the dominant culture. The difference is that individuals who are classified as acculturated are always identified as members of the minority

Jeffrey Mio, Lori Barker, and Melanie M. Domenech Rodriguez, from "Immigrants, Refugees, and the Acculturation Process," *Multicultural Psychology, 4th ed.*, pp. 166-168. Copyright © 2016 by Oxford University Press. Reprinted with permission.

culture, and they are relegated to a lower status and not completely accepted, even given their capabilities. Chao, Chen, Roisman, and Hong (2007) might call these individuals "bicultural essentialists" who believe that there is an essential quality to their ethnicity. Such individuals may experience more difficulties in switching between cultures than they consciously realize.

Another group defined by LaFramboise and associates (1993) is characterized by **fusion**. This idea is similar to the melting pot theory, wherein individuals come together to form a new, homogenous culture from parts of the different cultures. Fusion differs from Berry's assimilation group because aspects of multiple cultures are integrated into a new culture. Cultures of origin are not distinct and identifiable (LaFramboise et al., 1993). Fusion can sometimes be used as an excuse to "not see color" or other differences among people, which some people may argue is the perpetuating principle behind continuing racist acts.

A group that seems to have similarities with Berry's (1990, 1997) integrationist model is the **alternation** group (LaFramboise et al., 1993). This group regards two cultures as equal.

TABLE - LAFRAMBOISE AND ASSOCIATES' MODEL OF ACCULTURATION

Status	Brief Description
Assimilation	Absorption into the dominant culture
Acculturated	Competence in a second culture without complete acceptance
Fusion	The process of combining one's culture of origin with the host culture, creating a somewhat new culture
Alternation	The process of alternating between one's culture of origin and the host culture depending on what the context dictates
Multicultural	Distinct cultural identities are maintained with a single multicultural social structure

Source: LaFramboise, Coleman, and Gerton (1993).

An individual does not have to choose between the two cultures and can alter his or her behaviors to fit the context. LaFramboise and associates see this group as the optimal one, just as Berry (1990, 1997) describes the integrationist group as his most positive one. Though the alternation group is optimal and many people would wish to be able to adjust themselves according to context, this kind of life is not easy. It is not always possible to maintain positive relationships, even when an individual can adapt and adjust accordingly. However, there does seem to be some evidence that individuals can master this process (Devos, 2006).

> Alternation—competence in both the host culture and one's original culture such that one is able to apply the values and behaviors that are appropriate for the situation.

> Multicultural perspective—the perspective that there are multiple groups within a society and all groups are mutually appreciated.

The **multicultural group**, according to LaFramboise et al., (1993), involves cultures with distinct identities joined together within a social structure. Individuals from one culture cooperate with those of other cultures to serve common needs. This is different from the melting pot notion in that each subculture can maintain its identity while living among others without necessarily assimilating or completely adopting the others' cultures. This group may be more accurately described by Jesse Jackson's[1] pluralistic quilt idea, in which each culture can be seen apart from the others, yet are all joined within the "same blanket." This is the optimal and most extreme definition of the multicultural model. When there is interaction, however, there also tends to be mutual influence, and cultures of origin tend not to be distinctly maintained. Thus, the multicultural group is difficult to achieve in practice (LaFramboise et al., 1993).

The Berry and LaFramboise models of acculturation help us to determine the ways that people adapt to this society. These models could apply not only to immigrants and refugees but also to members of minority cultures who are trying to adapt successfully. However, as stated previously, the process of acculturation and the success of immigrants who are attempting to adjust to a new culture can be determined by their experiences before, during, and after their arrival in the host country.

---

[1] In his 1988 presidential campaign, Jesse Jackson described "a quilt of many colors" sewn by his grandmother. He said that a single patch of color was not large enough to provide warmth but that when it was combined with other patches of color, the result was a quilt that could keep someone warm and safe.

Once in their host countries, both immigrants and refugees may feel pressure to acculturate to their new surroundings. Mio, Barker, and Rodriquez (2016) said the following about immigrants and refugees and their acculturation process: "The degree to which immigrants and refugees successfully adjust to their host culture depends upon the degree to which they can successfully negotiate the blending of their traditional values with the new values of their host cultures." This is no small task to merge two different lives and ideologies together to fit a new environment.

Immigrants and refugees face challenges such as language barriers, new family roles, and lack of employment and educational opportunities. We should be aware of and appreciate these very daunting challenges. As mentioned before, there are many ways (some of them very simple) to help those trying to adjust to their new surroundings, and we can be an integral part of making their acculturation process less traumatizing and more meaningful.

Chapter 12

Multi-Cultural Competence

*The world in which you were born is just **one** model of reality. Other cultures are not failed attempts at being **you**: they are unique manifestations of the **human spirit**.*

—Wade Davis

Figure 12.1

"The beauty of the world lies in the diversity of its people."

-Unknown

What can we do to adjust our attitudes and behaviors to increase our understanding and respect for other cultures? Why do we have a hard time leaving our own circles? There are many reasons for this, but none of which are too hard to overcome and change for the better. When we focus on similarities and not differences, this alone can change our mind-set and provide a strong base for becoming more accepting of cultural differences.

WHY DO WE STRUGGLE WITH DIFFERENCES?

Becoming more multi-culturally competent is a topic that is discussed in depth by Mio, Barker, and Rodriguez (2016) in their book *Multicultural Psychology*. They have explained the 5 D's of Difference and the 3 S's of Similarities and why we, as humans, tend to struggle with coming together and what we can do to change this. Harrell (1995) explains people's reactions to situations in which they feel different. They are *distancing, denial, defensiveness, devaluing,* and *discovery.*

DISTANCING

Distancing is when we avoid situations in which we feel different. Mio et. al. (2016) say the following about distancing.

> If we do not get too close to the difference, the possibility of negative experiences is minimized. Distancing can occur physically, emotionally, and intellectually. We may avoid going into situations in which we know we will be different. Many people do this by always hanging out with people of similar backgrounds. OR, once we are in a situation in which we feel different, we may get out of there as soon as we can.

DENIAL

Well intentioned people, when encountering situations that are different or unfamiliar, may **deny** that there are any differences at all. Involved with this is pretending not to see the difference, minimizing its importance, or ignoring it altogether. It's important to understand that we all have things in common; however, denying differences can be negative by causing others to "feel invisible, ignored, discounted, and unimportant, and that limits the ability to have meaningful, enriching interactions with one another." (Mio, Barker, and Rodriguez 2016).

DEFENSIVENESS

To protect ourselves, we tend to be **defensive.** Unfamiliar experiences with others can be perceived as threatening which leads to other emotions such as discomfort, tension, and fear. Many times, those who feel this threat will claim that they are not bothered at all by differences. In fact, it's hard to find anyone who will actually admit that he or she is bothered by differences. That person may actually be doing and saying things that are opposite of what he or she is actually feeling. To admit to feelings of racism would be a threat to self-image.

DEVALUING

We tend to **devalue** others who are different and unfamiliar because it makes us feel more comfortable about ourselves. When we devalue (see things as deficient or less than,) we feel less threatened. Our natural tendency as human beings is to preserve and increase our self-esteem, so it is natural to place ourselves higher than another person. You may notice this when trying a new food from a different part of the world. Most of us will immediately turn our nose up at the thought of it, without even trying it. "Why would I eat something like that?" or "Who would ever want to eat that?" may be some statements used to devalue the ways and customs of others.

DISCOVERY

This aspect of the five differences is more positive. Experiences we have with others from different cultures can be an opportunity for **discovery.** Rather than avoid situations that are unfamiliar, we work through our anxiety and we see it as an opportunity for growth.

Figure 12.2a-b We want to feel comfortable with who we know and what we know, which makes it a challenge to step outside of our closest circles.

Copyright © Depositphotos/wavebreakmedia.   *Copyright © Depositphotos/Monkeybusiness.*

This entails stepping outside of our comfort zone, which is difficult for most of us to do. It's important to keep in mind that negative feelings associated with differences are normal and natural. Becoming aware of these feelings and taking steps to change them can enrich our lives. We can make a conscious effort to change our thinking patterns about differences, and when we expose ourselves to differences, they become more familiar which, in turn, leads to less prejudice and bias.

OUR DESIRE FOR SIMILARITY

The 3 S's of Similarity, according to Mio, Barker, and Rodriguez (2016), are that things are more *simple, safe,* and *sane.*

SIMPLE

It's just simple to stick with what we know and what is familiar. We have to work harder in situations that are uncomfortable and new. We want to feel comfortable! Who seeks situations that are uneasy? We want to be surrounded by others who share our values.

SAFE

As stated earlier, when things are different and unfamiliar, they can be perceived as a threat. When we are around our own group that has similar practices and values, we feel safe and protected.

SANE

We feel normal in our own environment. We begin to question ourselves and who we are when surrounded by everyone else who is different. We begin to feel that our behaviors, very familiar and comfortable to us, are wrong especially when surrounded by others who may not understand them. Being around others who are like us confirms to us that we are okay, and we feel validated. Beverly Daniel Tatum, author of *Why Are All the Black Kids Sitting Together in the Cafeteria?* (1997) points out that groups coming together is important to racial identity development. It's not that these students are trying to be exclusive or insulting rather just a way to feel "safe" and "sane" with those who share similarities and cultural norms.

POSITIVE STEPS TO BRIDGE CULTURAL GAPS

When working with others from another culture, there are some simple things we can do to make a positive relationship and allow for comfortable and positive experiences. Morris and Maisto, authors of *Understanding Psychology* (2016), suggest three strategies to reduce prejudice and discrimination. They are recategorization, controlled processing, and improving contact between groups.

STRATEGIES FOR REDUCING PREJUDICE AND DISCRIMINATION

The first is **recategorization.** This means that instead of focusing on differences, we can categorize unfamiliar people or situations into something that we can understand or with which we can better relate. The example given by Morris and Maisto involves religious differences such as Catholics and Protestants. Rather than being separate competing groups, they be put in the category as Christians. This can definitely change our schema to be more inclusive and understanding rather than different and separate.

The second strategy is **controlled processing.** Just as is the case with anything else in life, we can practice becoming more mindful of our own views and judgements about others. When we train ourselves to become more mindful of differences, we can also be aware of the biased attitudes that accompany them.

The third strategy is simply **improving contact between groups** for equal cooperation and positive contact between groups. There are a few conditions, however, that these contacts must have in order to be positive and effective.

1. Group members must have equal status.

2. People need to have one-on-one contact with members of the other group.

3. Members of the two groups must cooperate rather than compete.

LEARNING ABOUT OUR OWN CULTURE

We must ask ourselves how our own culture affects our personal attitudes and behaviors. It's important to understand ourselves and our thoughts and feelings about our own group. Some may say things such as "I don't have a culture," "I'm boring," or "I come from a family with no culture." These are statements I hear often in the classroom as we begin to identify and discuss what makes us who we are. Lori A. Barker (2016) suggests that statements such as these are egocentric in nature because it says that your own culture is the norm, and everyone else is different or abnormal. It means you use your own culture as a standard to measure others. For those who identify as being an American despite of ethnicity, then what does it mean to be an American? (Mio, Barker, and Rodriguez 2016).

UNDERSTANDING WORLDVIEWS

It's very important to learn about other cultures just as it is to understand your own. Obtaining a basic knowledge of other groups of people is a huge step toward multi-cultural competence. We need to understand that each individual person within any group is unique, but it's still helpful to understand basic facts such as history, sociopolitical views, traditions, family structure, and core values and beliefs (Mio, Barker, and Rodriguez 2016).

Travel is fatal to prejudice.

—Mark Twain

CONCRETE ACTIVITIES TO BUILD MULTI-CULTURAL COMPETENCE

Being aware of our own culture and taking steps to understand other cultures is important, but where do we begin? Mio, Barker, and Rodriguez (2016) have encouraged the following activities to increase interpersonal skills and levels of empathy and understanding for people from different backgrounds.

- Take more classes, attend lectures, workshops, seminars, and retreats on multicultural issues.

- Read books, magazines, and journals on multi-cultural issues.

- Watch relevant films and television shows on diverse issues.

- Listen to music and attend plays, concerts, and other cultural events and celebrations.

- Develop relationships with people from diverse backgrounds.

- Get involved in cultural organizations.

- Develop the ability to say "I don't know" and to ask questions. You cannot possibly know everything, so allow others to help you develop your knowledge.

- Travel to experience different cultures directly.

- Be an ally, and speak up on behalf of others.

- Speak up on behalf of yourself and your group.

- Develop a level of comfort discussing difficult issues.

- Have an attitude of discovery, and be open to new experiences.

- Have the courage to take risks, and step outside your comfort zone.

- Develop empathy for others, their experiences and perspectives.

CHANGING OUR WORLDVIEW

One of the greatest benefits I have as an instructor of Psychology and Culture is to hear from students about how much their views have changed and their eyes opened to different perspectives and attitudes around the world. Many of them begin to see who they are and how they view the world based on their own cultural backgrounds. Furthermore, many have felt more motivated to reach out, be more inclusive, and learn more about other cultures. They took some of the first steps by taking a class and becoming aware of psychology and how the cultural environment has a strong influence on who we are. They learned that what is different isn't necessarily wrong or right, just different ways to live.

Our small changes can contribute to larger cultural shifts in the end. By taking the information learned in this book and taking steps to increase our awareness, we can become an integral part of a great change. While understanding human similarities, we can also celebrate diversity and cultural differences that make our world colorful and amazing. This concluding quote by Desmond Tutu applies to this principle. He says, "Differences are not intended to separate, to alienate. We are different precisely in order to realize our need of one another." When we open our eyes and step outside of our own thoughts, attitudes, and beliefs to learn about others around the world, our own lives as well as the lives of others we encounter will be changed for the better.

Figure 12.3 This statement can seem overwhelming, but when we do our small part, we can make a positive change toward a greater goal of becoming unified, yet still able to celebrate cultural differences.

GLOSSARY

Absolutist (etic) approach—universal approach to human behavior. Psychologists supporting this view will argue that behavior and thought processes are basically the same in all cultures.

Accommodation—include or make space for new information, but not fully integrate it.

Acculturation—process of individual change and adaptation as a result of continuous contact with a new, distinct culture.

Acculturative stress—also known as 'culture shock.' A distressful psychological reaction to any unfamiliar cultural environment.

Actor-observer bias—the tendency to attribute our successes to our own efforts or qualities and our failures to external factors.

Assimilation—complete absorption into a new dominant culture.

Attribution theory—addresses the question of how people make judgements about the causes of behavior; internal and external.

Authoritarian parenting style—parents expect unquestioned obedience and view the child as needing to be controlled; they are low on warm and responsiveness. Children are found to be more anxious and withdraw as well as less positive.

Authoritative parenting style—parents are warm and nurturing as well as firm, fair and reasonable. This tends to be the most common. Children are found to have higher self-esteem. They are more positive and have higher social and emotional skills.

Barnum statement—statements that are overly inclusive of all humans. The willingness to accept these statements as truth is called the Barnum Effect. It's a 'one size fits all' type of thinking.

Belief perseverance—when one is unwilling to change their beliefs even when evidence proves different.

Bias—when one relies on vivid, but not necessarily accurate information about a person or a group of people.

Central symptoms—symptoms found globally in disorders.

Co-figurative culture—cultural change occurs more rapidly, adults continue to socialize their children but peers play a greater role in advice and information.

Cognition—conscious mental activity; activities of thinking, understanding, learning and remembering.

193

Collectivism—a social pattern in which individuals tend to be motivated by the group's or collective's preferences, needs and rights when they come into conflict with those of the individual.

Content validity—having an adequate sample of questions measuring the skills or knowledge the test is supposed to measure.

Continuous variable—varying degrees or shades of grey with almost everything we encounter in our experiences.

Criterion-based validity—validity measured by a comparison of the test score and independent measures of what the test is designed to measure.

Critical thinking—an active and systematic cognitive strategy to examine, evaluate and understand events, solve problems, and make decisions on the basis of sound reasoning and valued evidence.

Cross-cultural psychology—critical and comparative study of cultural effects on human psychology.

Culture—set of attitudes, behaviors and symbols shared by a large group of people and usually communicated from one generation to the next.

Culture-bound syndromes—psychological disorders usually observed with a specific culture. It is not something found globally.

Culture-fair tests—intelligence tests designed to eliminate cultural bias by minimizing the use of language as well as skills and values that vary from one culture to another.

Culture shock—see acculturative stress.

Defensive—unfamiliar experiences with others can be perceived as threatening, which leads to other emotions such as discomfort, tension and fear.

Defensive attribution—tendency to attribute our successes to our own efforts or qualities and our failures to external factors.

Denial—denying that there are differences between individuals or groups of people. This can have a negative effect by causing others to feel invisible, ignored, or unimportant.

Devalue—when we devalue (see things as deficient or less than) we feel less threatened.

Diagnostic and Statistical Manual of Mental Disorders—see *DSM-5*.

Direct communication—literal and assertive, e.g., "Let's go to dinner."

Discovery—rather than avoiding situations that are unfamiliar, we work though anxiety and see our connections with others from different backgrounds as an opportunity for growth.

Discrimination—a behavior; unfair act or acts directed against an entire group of people or individual members of that group.

Display rules—rules of emotional expression for a culture.

Distancing—avoiding situations in which we feel different.

DSM-5—The Diagnostic and Statistical Manual of Mental Disorders is the primary manual used by health and mental health professionals the United States to diagnose mental disorders. The *DSM* has gone through several revisions. The most current version is the *DSM-5*, which is the fifth edition.

Emotion—response that has some physiological arousal and cognitive interpretation and is followed by a behavioral expression.

Enculturation—product of the socialization process; subjective, underlying, psychological aspects of a culture that become internalized through development.

Ethnicity—indicates a cultural heritage; the experience shared by people who have a common ancestral origin, language, traditions, religions and often a geological territory.

Ethnocentrism—the view that supports judgements about other ethnic, national and cultural groups and events from the observer's own ethnic, national or cultural group's outlook.

Explicit cultural norms—when one can see a cultural norm by one's clothing or behavioral responses.

Extended family—grandparents, aunts, uncles, and/or cousins living together.

Flynn effect—IQ scores have increased in the population as a whole. Possible explanations include improvements made in nutrition and health care and that the population is better at test taking.

Foreign language processing difficulties—people who speak in a different language may draw negative impressions and stereotypes based on their response time and seem to have more cognitive difficulties while processing information.

Fundamental attribution error—the tendency for people to place an undue emphasis on internal characteristics rather than external factors when explaining another person's behavior in a given situation.

Gender—refers to behaviors that a culture deems appropriate for men and women.

Gender identity—the degree to which a person has awareness or recognition that he or she adopts a particular gender role.

Gender role—the degree to which a person adopts the gender-specific behaviors ascribed by his or her culture.

Globalization—the act of globalizing, which is extending to other parts of the world, by integrating and developing economies, philosophies and lifestyles.

Group tests—written intelligence tests administered by one examiner to many people at one time.

Human development—changes in physical, psychological and social behaviors that are experienced by individuals across the lifespan, from conception to death.

Immigrants—those who have made a choice to move to a new country for a better life or job opportunities.

Implicit cultural norms—cultural norms that are not readily seen such as expectations for behavior, bargaining, or any unwritten norms in day-to-day behavior.

Incidence—the number of new cases that arise in a given period.

Indigenous healing—encompasses therapeutic beliefs and practices that are rooted within a given culture.

Indigenous personalities—culture-specific personality traits.

Indirect communication—relies on context and the receiver's ability to draw inference. E.g. "Are you hungry? What's your favorite restaurant?"

Individualism—a social pattern in which individuals tend to motivated by their own preferences, needs and rights when they come into conflict with those of a group or collective in which the individual is a member.

Intelligence—a general term referring to the ability or abilities involved in learning and adaptive behavior.

Kinesics—bodily movements while communicating, e.g. hand gestures or body language.

Legal knowledge—knowing the form of laws and other prescriptions established by authorities from tribal or community leaders to a central government. Used by authorities and people themselves to pass judgements about psychological aspects of human behavior.

Lifetime incidence—the number of cases of a disorder that occur during one's lifetime.

Matriarchal society—a social system where females hold primary power and with the mother or oldest female as head of the family, tribe or clan.

Measures of central tendency—used to find where score distributions are located (mean, median, mode).

Mental disorder—a clinically significant behavior and psychological syndrome or pattern that occurs in an individual and is associated with present distress or disability, or with a significantly increased risk of suffering, death, pain, disability or important loss of freedom.

Meta-analysis—combining the results from several independent studies, then comparing for disagreements in data, research biases, research methods used and any other factors that contributed to the research conclusions.

Meta-thinking—when we think about the way we think and the way in which we categorize things in our environment.

Modern culture—see non-traditional culture.

Multicultural groups—involves cultures with distinct identities joined together within a social structure. Individuals from one culture cooperate with those of other cultures to serve common needs. This differs from the melting pot notion in that each subcultural can maintain its identity while living among others without necessarily assimilating or completely adopting the others' cultures.

Multiculturalism—psychological and theoretical view that encourages equality and supports the idea that cultural groups have the right to follow their own unique path.

Nation—people who share a common geographical origin, history and language but are also unified as a political entity; an independent state recognized by other countries.

Nationality—the status of belonging to a particular nation; a group forming a part of one of more political nations.

Non-traditional culture—also known as a modern culture; constantly shifting and changing with new ideas and principles that are usually based on scientific and technical developments.

Paralanguage—nonverbal vocal cues in conversation such as silence, loudness of voice, rates of speech, etc.

Patriarchal society—A social system in which the father is the head of the family; a community or society is governed mostly by men.

Perception—the way in which our sensations are processed and organized in our brain.

Performance tests—intelligence tests that minimize the use of language.

Peripheral symptoms—symptoms from a disorder found in specific cultures and only in those cultures.

Permissive parenting style—very low parental guidelines. The parents are warm and loving, but allow their children to regulate their own lives. Children tend to be rebellious and lacking direction.

Post-figurative culture—cultural change is slow and socialization occurs primarily by elders transferring their knowledge to their children.

Pre-figurative culture—the culture is changing so rapidly that young people may be the ones to teach the adults. The knowledge that adults hold may be insufficient for the next generation, and adults may need to look to younger people for advice and information.

Prejudice—an attitude; unfair, intolerable or unfavorable views of a group of people.

Prevalence—the frequency with which a given disorder occurs at a given time.

Primacy effect—occurs when early information about someone weighs more heavily than later information in influencing one's impression of that person.

Proxemics—personal space in conversation.

Psychometric equivalence—the degree to which instruments used in the cultures participating in the research measure the same construct.

Psychotherapy—the treatment of a psychological disorder through psychological means and usually involves having verbal interaction with a licensed therapist.

Qualitative research—conducted primarily in a natural setting; used when trying to discuss psychological phenomena like dreams, pictures, songs, drawings or any topic for which standardized measurements aren't suitable or available.

Quantitative research—measures data, for example: quantity, degree, magnitude, measures of central tendency and/or correlational coefficients.

Race—genetically transmitted physical characteristics that a specific group of people share.

Recategorization—instead of focusing on differences, we can recategorize unfamiliar people or situations into something that we can understand or with which we can better relate.

Refugees—those who have been forced to flee their homeland because of a threat to their life or safety, or who fear persecution. Most do not choose where they will do and are most often unable to return to their own country.

Relativist perspective—human beings develop ideas, establish behavioral norms and learn emotional responses according to a set of cultural prescriptions. Therefore, people from different cultural settings should understand psychological disorders differently and the differences should be significant. It is called 'relativist' because it puts psychological phenomena into a relative perspective.

Relativistic (emic) approach—psychologists supporting this view say that human behavior in its full complexity can be understood only within the context of the culture in which it occurs.

Reliability—the ability of a test to produce consistent and stable scores.

Religious affiliation—and individual's acceptance of knowledge, beliefs and practices related to a particular faith.

Schema—a cognitive structure that organizes our thoughts, knowledge, beliefs, and past experiences providing a framework to understand new events and experiences.

Schemata—organized sets of beliefs and expectations based on past experience that is presumed to apply to all members of that category.

Schizophrenic disorders—severe disorders in which there are disturbances of thoughts, communications, and emotions. Symptoms include hallucinations, delusions, and being out of touch with reality (psychotic).

Self-fulfilling prophecy—when a person's expectations about another elicits behavior from the second person that confirms the expectation.

Sensation—receptor cells are stimulated and sent to our brains to be processed.

Sensory adaptation—the tendency of the sensory system to response less to stimuli that continue without change.

Sex—refers to the physical characteristics and differences between males and females.

Sex roles—used to describe behaviors that males and females may engage in that are directly related to their biological differences and the process of reproduction.

Sexual identity—used to describe the awareness and recognition of sex and sex roles an individual has.

Shaman—traditional healers and doctors (especially in under-developed countries) who use native healing as a primary source of healthcare.

Socialization—the process by which we learn and internalize the rules and patterns of the society in which we live; mastering societal norms.

Society—composed of people living together in an ordered community.

Somatization—expression of psychological symptoms through physical symptoms.

Stanford-Binet intelligence scale—the first test developed to measure intelligence yielding and intelligence quotient (IQ).

Traditional culture—based on the traditions, rules and patterns of living that have been set by past generations.

Uninvolved parenting style—the parents are too involved in their own lives and merely care for their children's physical needs while paying little to no attention to them. In the extreme form, this is parental neglect. Children from this style fare the worst. Many turn to drugs and crime and have low self-esteem.

Universalist perspective—despite the cultural differences, people have a great number of similar features, including attitudes, values and behavioral responses. Therefore, the overall understanding of mental disorders ought to be universal. It is called 'universal' because it suggests the existence of absolute, invariable symptoms of psychopathology across cultures.

Validity—the ability of a test to measure what it's been designed to measure.

Wechsler intelligence scale—measures verbal and performance abilities and also yields an overall IQ score.

Worldview—a philosophy on life or the way we perceive the world that affects the way we feel, think, behave and how we interact with others.

REFERENCES

Acioly, N. M. & Schliemann, A. D. (1986). Intuition, mathematics & schooling in understanding a lottery game. *Paper presented at the Tenth PME conference, London.*

Alain Corcos (1997). "The Myth of Human Races" 144–146. Michigan State University Press. Triandis, H. C. (1995). *Individualism and Collectivism.* Boulder, Co. Westview.

Bolzman, C., Fibbi, R., & Vial, M. (2006). What to do after retirement? Elderly migrants and the question of return. *Journal of Ethnic and Migration Studies, 32* (8), 1359–1375.

Buss, D. M. (1994) *Sexual strategies: The evolution of human mating.* New York: Basic Books.

Cheal, B. (2001). Refugees and immigrants have different experiences. Available at http://teachersworkshop.org/experiences.pdf.

Consedine, N., & Magai, C. (2002). The uncharted waters of emotion: Ethnicity, trait emotion and emotional expression in older adults. *Journal of Cross-Cultural Gerontology,* 17 (1), 71–100.

Dinges, N. G. & Hull, P. (1992). Personality, culture and international studies, In D. Lieberman (Ed.), *Revealing the world: for interdisciplinary reader for international studies.* Dubuque, IA: Kendall-Hunt.

Gladwin, H., & Gladwin, C. (1971). Estimating market conditions and profit expectations of fish sellers at Cape Coast, Ghana. In G. Dalton (Ed), *Studies in Economic Anthropology* (Anthropological Studies No. 7, pp. 122–143).

Gladwin, T. (1970). *East is a big bird: Navigation and Logic on Puluwat Atoll.* Cambridge, MA: Harvard University Press.

Goldsten, D., Molock, S., Whitbeck, L., Murakami, J., Zayas, L., & Hall, C. G. N. (2008). Cultural considerations in adolescent suicide prevention and psychosocial treatment. *American Psychologist, 63* (1), 14–31.

Harrell, S.P. (1995). Dynamics of Difference: Personal and sociocultural dimensions of intergroup relations. *Paper presented at the 103rd Annual Convention of the American Psychological Association, New York.*

Hoffstede, G. H., & Bond, M. (1984). Hofestede's cultural dimensions: An independent validation using Rokeach's value survey, *Journal of Cross-Cultural Psychology, 15,* 417–433.

Hull, P. V. (1987). Bilingualism: Two languages, two personalities? *Resources in Education, educational resources clearinghouse on education.* Ann Arbor: University of Michigan Press.

Krumov, K. & Larsen, K. S., (2013). *Cross-Cultural Psychology: Why Culture Matters.* Information Age Publishing.

Levy, R. I. (1973). *Tahitians.* Chicago: University of Chicago Press.

Li-Repac, D. (1980). Cultural influences on clinical perception: A comparison between Caucasian and Chinese-American therapists. *Journal of Cross-Cultural Psychology,* 11, 327–342.

Maslow, A. (1970). *Motivation & Personality (2nd Ed).* New York: Harper & Row.

Markus, H. R., & Kitayama, S. (1998). The cultural psychology of personality. *Journal of Cross-Cultural Psychology, 29* (1), 63–87.

Mead, Margaret (1978). *Culture & Commitment.* Garden City, NY: Anchor.

Morris, M. H., Avila, R. A., & Allen, J. (1993). Individualism and the modern corporation: Implications for innovation and entrepreneurship. *Journal of Management,* 19 (3), 595–612.

Nyambegera, S. M., Daniels, K., & Sparrow, P. (2001). Why fit doesn't always matter: The impact of HRM and cultural fit on job involvement of Kenyan employees, *Applied.*

Okazaki, S. Liu, J., Longworth, S., & Minn, J. (2002). Asian American-White American differences in expressions of social anxiety; a replication and extension. *Cultural Diversity and Ethnic Minority Psychology, 8* (3), 234–247.

Reisman, P. (1977). *Freedom in Falani social life: An introspective ethnography* (M. Fuller, Trans). Chicago; University of Chicago Press. (Original work published 1974).

Russell, G. L., Fujino, D. C., Sue, S., Cheung, M., & Snowden L. R. (1996). The effects of the therapist-client ethnic match in the assessment of mental health functioning. *Journal of Cross-Cultural Psychology, 27 (5) 598–615.*

Scherer, K. R. & Walbott, H. (1994). Evidence for universality and cultural variation of differential emotion response patterning. *Journal of Personality and Social Psychology, 66,* 310–328.

Snyder, M., & Swann, W. B., Jr. (1978) Behavioral confirmation in social interaction: From Social Perception to social reality. *Journal of Experimental Social Psychology, 14,* 148–162.

Sue, D. W. & Sue, D. (2007). *Counseling the culturally diverse: theory and practice Fifth edition.* New York: John Wiley & Sons.

Tatum, B. D. (1997). *"Why are all the Black kids sitting together in the cafeteria?" and other conversations about race.* New York; Boise Books.

Triandis, H. C., (2001). Individualism and collectivism: Past, present, and future. In D. Matsumoto (ed.), *Handbook of Culture and Psychology* (pp. 35–50).

Van den bos, K., Brockner, J., Stein, J., Steiner, D. D., Van Yperen, N. W., & Dekker, D.M. (2013). The psychology of voice and performance capabilities in masculine and feminine cultures and contexts. *Journal of Personality & Psychology.*

Williams, J. E. & Best, D. L. (1990). *Measuring sex stereotypes: A multinational study.* Newbury, CA: Sage Publications.

CPSIA information can be obtained
at www.ICGtesting.com
Printed in the USA
FSOW02n1617281117
41717FS